2007
A POETRY ODYSSEY

After a voyage of 2,500 years, poetry has finally reached the stars ...

Leicestershire
Edited by Donna Samworth

First published in Great Britain in 2007 by:
Young Writers
Remus House
Coltsfoot Drive
Peterborough
PE2 9JX
Telephone: 01733 890066
Website: www.youngwriters.co.uk

All Rights Reserved

© Copyright Contributors 2007

SB ISBN 978-1 84602 811 3

Foreword

This year, the Young Writers' *2007: A Poetry Odyssey* competition proudly presents a showcase of the best poetic talent selected from thousands of up-and-coming writers nationwide.

Young Writers was established in 1991 to promote the reading and writing of poetry within schools and to the young of today. Our books nurture and inspire confidence in the ability of young writers and provide a snapshot of poems written in schools and at home by budding poets of the future.

The thought, effort, imagination and hard work put into each poem impressed us all and the task of selecting poems was a difficult but nevertheless enjoyable experience.

We hope you are as pleased as we are with the final selection and that you and your family continue to be entertained with *2007: A Poetry Odyssey Leicestershire* for many years to come.

Contents

Abington High School
- Kate Lowther (13) — 1
- Emily Vale (13) — 2
- Chloe Palmer (13) — 3
- Kelly Biffen (13) — 4
- Sophie Johnson (13) — 5
- Sian Byrne (14) — 6
- Evangeline Hirst (13) — 7
- Amy Stewart (13) — 8
- Charlie O'Neill (13) — 9
- Emily Panteli (13) — 10
- Emily Coulson & Kayleigh Walker (14) — 11
- Rachel Oliver (13) — 12
- Franchesca Towers (13) — 13
- Tom Brown (14) — 14
- Ashley Hayes (13) — 15
- Kelly Weston (12) — 16
- Tanya Wilson (12) — 17
- Taranjet Dhinsa (14) — 18
- Lucy Kendall (12) — 19
- Paige Gray (12) — 20
- James Sarson (12) — 21
- Myles Crutchley (12) — 22
- Iwanna Hackett (12) — 23
- Sharanjeet Dhinsa (12) — 24
- Gary Stephens (12) — 25
- Gulsen Tosun (12) — 26
- Alex Nicholson (13) — 27
- Clare Abbott (14) — 28

Ashfield School
- Aasiya Alana (16) — 29

Crown Hills Community School
- Shazeena Majothi (12) — 30
- Zainab Adam (12) — 31
- Ravi Maher (13) — 32
- Altamash Nazirahamed (12) — 33

Ellesmere College
- Amy Vertigan (14) — 34
- John Madgwick (14) — 35
- Hannah Khan (14) — 36
- Areefa Khan (14) — 37
- Rebecca D'Souza (14) — 38

English Martyrs School
- Conor Beattie (12) — 39
- Matthew Walne (11) — 40
- Bernadette Woodley (11) — 41
- Gee-won Park (11) — 42
- Melissa Law (12) — 43
- Keanu Sherriff-Geary (11) — 44
- Suzanna Newton (11) — 45
- Emily Gaskin (11) — 46
- Anu Joseph (11) — 47
- Rebecca Fenn (12) — 48
- Emily Sherman (11) — 49
- Ben Shaw (11) — 50
- Shylet Muza (11) — 51
- Daniel Williamson (11) — 52
- Aaron Gibbard (11) — 53
- Roberta Cooley (11) — 54
- Aidan Fisher (11) — 55
- Matthew Malone (11) — 56
- Brenna Benjamin (11) — 57
- Marlyce Pepe-Ngoma (11) — 58
- George Muller (11) — 59
- Joshua Saunders (12) — 60
- Gabrielle Flood (11) — 61
- Junior Manun'Ebo (11) — 62
- Chloe Randall (12) — 63
- Connell Smyth (11) — 64
- Jack Snart (11) — 65
- Christian Kamara (11) — 66
- Amy Day (11) — 67
- Thomas Lloyd-Jones (12) — 68
- Abigail Leader (11) — 69
- Olivia Norris (12) — 70
- Abigail Kearney (11) — 71

George Richards (11) — 72
Emily White (11) — 73
Robert Law (11) — 74
Rhianna Stretton (11) — 75
Charlotte Richardson (11) — 76
Joanna Uczniak (11) — 77
Connor Wickwar (11) — 78
James Fernandez-Harrison (11) — 79
Jak Skelly (11) — 80
Charlotte Waite (11) — 81
Lydon D'Costa (11) — 82
Hannah O'Neill (12) — 83
Joseph Stoneleigh (12) — 84
Keira Wall (13) — 85
Tasmin Kennedy (12) — 86
Fern Watkins (12) — 88
Gabrielle Parkinson (12) — 90
Gee-Young Park (12) — 91
Olivia Cluskey (12) — 92
Laura McLoughlin (12) — 93
Jacob Brown (12) — 94
Daniel Leung (12) — 95
Vienna Bradley (11) — 96
Jessica Dawson (11) — 97
Daniel Desewu (12) — 98

Garendon High School

Matthew Gilmore (12) — 99
Josh Nicholls (12) — 100
Jessica Thorpe (12) — 101
Dominic Cunliffe (12) — 102
Hannah Johnston (12) — 103
Josh Platts (12) — 104
Lauren O'Connell (12) — 105
Stephanie Willis (12) — 106
Michael Meyerstein (12) — 107
Tejal Patel (12) — 108
Calum Kirk (11) — 109
Charlotte Jones (11) — 110
Alex Thomas (11) — 111
Lydia Brown (13) — 112

Megan McTavish (11)	113
Matthew Bassett (11)	114
Megan Bass (11)	115
Samantha Tyler (11)	116
Elizabeth Callan (12)	117
Christopher Mitchell (11)	118
Callum Bowley (11)	119
Abigail Lee (11)	120
Ashton Allen (11)	121
Emma Wright (11)	122
Will Roe (11)	123
Louise Cox (11)	124
Laith Al-Samawi (11)	125
Giorgia Francis (12)	126
Tomasz Williams (12)	127
Sarah Blanchard (11)	128
Mayank Patel (11)	129
Darren Smith (11)	130
Krishan Patel (11)	131
Thomas Skillen (11)	132
Stuart Davis (11)	133
Corey Muncie (11)	134
Rebecca Smith (11)	135
Zoe Wooldridge (12)	136
Sarah Bajor (11)	137
Chloe Lazell (11)	138
Emmie Bradshaw (11)	139
Leon Caine (11)	140
Emma Willis (11)	141
Karishma Purshottam (11)	142
James Bullock (12)	143
Nikita Thompson (11)	144
Liam Start (12)	145
Alastair Hawkins (13)	146
Elizabeth Hickman (13)	147
Shannon Checkley (13)	148
Christopher Reeves (13)	149
Melissa Tombs (13)	150
Sam Haghighat (13)	151
Daniel Day (13)	152
Matthew Sanders (11)	153
Sean Woolley (11)	154

Mount Grace High School
Hollie Cartwright (11)   155
Jacob Watson (11)   156
Katherine Harris (14)   157
Joshua Stubberfield (12)   158
Katie MacNaughton (14)   159
Kelly Ward (13)   160
Danielle Smith (11)   161
Lorna Pacey (11)   162
Amy Pacey (13)   163
Taylor Crisp (11)   164

The Rutland College
Rebecca Hindmarch (16)   165
Natasha Schofield (16)   166
Keri Mowat (16)   167
Chris White (18)   168
Amii Slater (16)   169
Elizabeth Blades (16)   170
Cheryl Freestone (17)   172
David Rattenbury (17)   173
Marc Garley (16)   174
Sophie Morgan (16)   175
Rebecca Williams (16)   176
Sean Goff (16)   177
Graham Nice (17)   178
Gemma Ryan (16)   179
Anna Diffey (16)   180
Phoebe Harris (16)   181
Amy Bell (16)   182
Alan Young (18)   183
Jennifer Griggs (16)   184
Carly Brown (17)   185
Maria Walmsley (16)   186
Matt Howlett (16)   187

The Poems

For You

The wind blows softly through the trees, grass and flowers.
I remember in the summer we would make daisy chains for hours.
It was so relaxing; it took all our stress away,
Then someone would come over and want me to go and play.

Some roses are red and some violets are blue
But there is a big bunch of flowers and the big red rose is you.

You were cheerful and happy and never wore a frown
Because nothing in the world would ever make you down.

We all miss you and you know it's true
So for every song, letter or poem, I will dedicate to you.

Kate Lowther (13)
Abington High School

My Dream

It was a long time ago.
I remember . . .
The big, tall house covered in snow.
I remember . . .
The little songbirds freezing on trees.
I remember . . .
The jangling sound of freezing keys
I remember . . .
The old frosted snowman, his scarf on the ground.
I remember . . .
All I hear is nothing but a soft sound.
I remember . . .
His top hat wonky from blustered winds.
I remember . .
Smashed glass from empty bottles of gin.
I remember . . .

It was a long time ago
I remember . . .
Frosted-up canal no longer a-flow.
I remember . . .
The place is deserted, no one around.
I remember . . .
All I can hear is nothing, but a soft sound.
That is all I remember!

Emily Vale (13)
Abington High School

School

Here I am
Sitting at my desk,
I'm not sure what to do,
I'm making a mess.
Scribbles and crosses
All over my book,
I better get a move on
The teacher's coming to look.
Thinking as much as I possibly can
I'm not quite as clever as they think I am.
Sometimes I wonder why we have these schools
Full of work and stupid rules.
'No chewing gum, no make-up, shirts in,' they say
I'm so happy when it's the end of the day!

Chloe Palmer (13)
Abington High School

Snowflakes

Cold to touch, we melt in your hand,
We look so soft but we're not on land.
You'll slip and slide
When through the night we glide.

We build up and up, we're three-feet deep,
In the morning you hear the cars beep.
Glistening in the moonlight
You know the next morning will be bright.

There will be water all about
When the sun comes out.
The snowmen will melt
When all the snow is dealt.

We just can't wait for the next day
That we can come out and play.
Everywhere is becoming clear
We've finished for another year.

Kelly Biffen (13)
Abington High School

Clouds

I sail through the sky
Like a ship on the waves.
I let out my tears
Which I have had to save.

I have been through good
And I have been through bad.
I have seen the world
Some of it makes me sad!

I am so very happy
When the sun comes out.
It makes me sing
It makes me shout.

I skip, I dance,
I shout hip hip *hooray!*
I hope the sun
Comes out every day!

I am happy now
But my day is done.
I have been fluffy and light
Like a hot cross bun.

Sophie Johnson (13)
Abington High School

Seaside Love

I'm going to the seaside,
To catch myself a tan.
Running round, meeting lads,
And sleeping on the sand.

Unpacking at the hotel,
Thank God I'm finally here,
Going in my private fridge
To get myself a beer.

Walking to the fairground,
Having lots of fun,
Eating loads of candyfloss,
This day has just begun.

Back at the hotel,
Jumping in the shower,
My hotel room is so grand,
It gives me a sense of power.

The second day of my holiday,
Everything's going great,
Last night I met a hot guy,
Who's taking me on a date.

Now I know he's decent,
He leans in for a kiss,
I'm thinking, *should I or shouldn't I?*
Maybe I'll give it a miss!

I know I made the right choice,
I finally found true love
I found me a special guy
That's sent from up above.

Sian Byrne (14)
Abington High School

Brain Block

I have a brain block,
I can't think what to write,
That light bulb in my head just isn't bright.

I have a brain block,
My fingers are clicking,
But the clock in my head just isn't ticking.

I have a brain block,
I think I need saving,
That brain in my head just isn't waving.

I have a brain block,
There's no fireworks popping,
That penny in my head just isn't dropping.

I have a brain block,
Soon I'll be weeping,
That brain in my head really is sleeping.

I had a brain block but now
The light bulb is bright, the clock is ticking,
My brain is waving, the penny is dropping
And my brain's not sleeping!
Oh yeah and I've written this poem.

Evangeline Hirst (13)
Abington High School

Summer

It's summer already, what can I say?
I'm getting ready for a bright sunny day.
Everybody going down to the beach,
The fun is now within a small reach.

Palm trees swaying in the breeze,
Having fun in the cold seas,
Children splashing all around,
Building up sandcastles in a mound.

It's a summer's day, everybody's having fun,
For most, that's sunbathing in the sun,
Ice-cold lollies all around,
Not a jumper or coat to be found.

We've had a great day,
This is all I can say,
The sun has gone down
And we're ready to hit the town!

Amy Stewart (13)
Abington High School

English And Stuff

I can't think of anything to write,
My brain is trying with all its might.
I've been forced to write a poem about poems,
My hate for English is really showing.
By the end of this lesson I'll be asleep
I'll be silent as night, you won't hear a peep.

I'm starting to fall asleep; this lesson is so boring,
In half an hour you'll hear me snoring.
Jack is sitting next to me, reading a poem about May
This will be the stuff that sends me on my holiday.
The legendary 'Spooks' poem sounds great
He forever longs to be called my best mate . . .
But he's not!

So now you know about my hate for English,
But don't worry; this pointless poem is nearly finished.
Please don't let this poem put you off this subject,
After all, we've never even met.

Charlie O'Neill (13)
Abington High School

Is This Love?

What's the point of loving someone?
I don't see the point!
Kissing, hugging, holding hands
And sticking by the joint.
Is this love?

Walking on a moonlit beach
Or sitting in the sun,
Walking down a busy street
Or clubbing and having fun!
Is this love?

Sitting by an open fire
As close as you can be,
Sharing thoughts and their hearts desire
Try it and you will see,
This is love!

Emily Panteli (13)
Abington High School

Daddy's Little Girl

It's hard to believe that so long ago
That you hurt me and my family so,
A family destroyed because of you
Think of all the pain you put us through.

You never thought about our hopes and dreams
Just thought of yourself, well, that's how it seems,
One of the people that were supposed to protect me
Was the one who crashed me back down to reality.

Physical and emotional,
The pain was unbearable,
The memories one day we hope to forget,
But we hope losing us is something you'll regret.

The story of sorrow
That we live to tell,
The story goes on without you
And all the hell.

We were just children,
We had innocent eyes,
But you showed us the violence
And all the lies.

You cheated and lied,
Against the role models of our lives,
You shattered our world, but before that
We were Daddy's little girls.

Emily Coulson & Kayleigh Walker (14)
Abington High School

The Wind

When the wind is happy,
It blows a gentle breeze.
When the wind is cold,
It begins to sneeze.
When the wind is angry,
It blows a hurricane.
Then the sun comes out,
And it's happy again.

Rachel Oliver (13)
Abington High School

Diesel

Diesel is my crazy, lazy, cuddly dog,
He loves to play tag
And eat my favourite bag.

He likes jumping in muddy puddles
And he loves lots of cuddles.

Diesel my dog hates his brush
And usually runs off in a rush.

At the end of the day when I give him a cuddle
I look at his fur . . . oh what a muddle!

Franchesca Towers (13)
Abington High School

I Hate Poetry

I hate poetry every day
I hate it when it is about how people play
I hate poetry
I hate it every day
So why, oh why, am I writing poetry today?

I hate it when people speak of their poetry
I hate it when they sing and shout,
'Look at my poetry'
So why, oh why, do I listen to poetry?

I bet now you think
Why, oh why, is he writing poetry
And why, oh why is he telling us his poetry?
I'll tell you why and show you why, because secretly
I love poetry!

Tom Brown (14)
Abington High School

My TV

The magic box in my front room
That sends and sounds like *kaboom!*
The box that shows people and places
And shows commercials for Macy's!

These commercials can be annoying
And they are always deploying
The amount of money spent on these things
Can have a permanent dent on your savings!

This box is where celebrities are made
And celebrity fat fighters drive my rage
They say you can't eat anything with fat
And say that you should instead eat your cat!

However, the box is the best
It's better than the rest
Although it may not be written
The TV is the heart of Britain.

Ashley Hayes (13)
Abington High School

Bye-Bye Bunny Boy

Bye-bye bunny boy
It's time to say goodnight.
I'm feeding you to crocodiles
You'll have to put up a fight.
Crocs go munch
Your bones will go crunch
So bye-bye bunny boy
You're heading towards the light!

Kelly Weston (12)
Abington High School

Ice Skates

I know myself as ice skates.
I feel heavy and smooth like ice.
I hear the scratch of the floor and the cheer of the crowd.
I see pretty dresses, blue ones, pink ones, red ones and black ones.
I am here to have fun and be number one.
I have a blade as sharp as a knife
And I have a shiny life.
I also know how to fly and jump real high.

Tanya Wilson (12)
Abington High School

Simple Friends, Good Friends

Friends are people that are always up for sharing
A real friend wouldn't make you do anything daring.
Friends always go through happiness and sadness
Then always let you know their gladness.

A simple friend might break up
But wouldn't exactly, like a good friend, want to make up.
A simple friend is someone that thinks of you just as a friend
But a real friend loves you and likes your trends.

A simple friend wouldn't want to get involved
In arguments you have with anything that can be solved.
A real friend would always stick by your side
But a simple friend wouldn't want you to fail any pride.

Friends, friends, friends, almost everyone has
If you don't have friends you can't have a laugh.
Friends are people that tell you their close secrets
But simple friends don't keep the promises and go tell.

Good friends are always there when you need them
But a simple friend to help would only say, 'Um!'

Taranjet Dhinsa (14)
Abington High School

September

S hiny leaves are good to see
E xcept the fog because you can't see
P eople love playing in leaves
T he frost glistens like snow
E ating hot lunch keeps us warm
M y special trees have no leaves
B ack to school, good job, I like school
E asy to keep warm in my house
R eady to leave summer behind.

Lucy Kendall (12)
Abington High School

September

S ome days it gets cold like ice
E veryone goes to the shops buying their uniform
P eople starting to stay indoors more
T rees are bare with no leaves
E very day people get frustrated
M ums have tons more washing
B rown leaves being crumpled on the floor
E verywhere you go, it's as cold as a freezer
R unning boys trying to keep warm.

Paige Gray (12)
Abington High School

Chocolate

C hunky as a chip
H ollow chocolate is the best
O range-flavoured
C runchie
O h so delicious
L ooks lovely
A s brown as the earth
T astes better
E xciting feeling down my mouth.

James Sarson (12)
Abington High School

My Favourite Console

eX tremely the best game's console in the shops
 B etter than the PS2
 O bviously the best game graphics
eX citingly fun to play on

 3 60 pounds for the full version
 6 00 or more have been sold in the United Kingdom
 0 h, cool.

Myles Crutchley (12)
Abington High School

Electric Guitar

I know myself as candy burst guitar,
I feel hard and metallic,
I hear my strings strum like I could sing,
One million and one lyrics.

My colours are pink or candy,
Then it fades to white,
And if someone comes in the room at night,
They can see me because I'm so right.

My purpose is to make brilliant sound
And make most people happy.
But if I was ever moved from my owner's room
I'm sure she'd go wappy!

My key features are my strings which make me what I am
Without these I would be thrown away
Just like an old used can.

All I know is how to play songs,
I can't do anything else,
So that's why without me,
My owner could do nothing else.

So right now I am happy here
I hit her happiness like a dart,
When I'm not being played I kind of feel sad
But I'll always have a place in her heart.

Iwanna Hackett (12)
Abington High School

Caught A Little Rhyme

Once upon a time
I caught a little rhyme.
I set it on the floor
And it ran right out the door.
I caught it on my bicycle
And it turned into a tricycle
Then it melted into an icicle.
I soaked it into my hat
But it turned into a cat.
Then it turned into a boat
I hopped into my boat
But it turned into a goat.
I fed it tin and paper
And it turned into a skyscraper!

Sharanjeet Dhinsa (12)
Abington High School

Eyes On The Ball

I run down the pitch
Looking for the ball,
I turn around,
I hear a call.

I run, run as fast as I can,
And play the ball straight through the wing,
I'm stunned,
As a light comes from this hefty bling.

I see the ball,
I run towards it,
I take my aim
I'm ready to hit.

I pull my leg back
And hear a crack,
I hit with all my might
Goal!

Gary Stephens (12)
Abington High School

I Know Myself

I know myself as a bed.
Feeling heavy as a car,
Also soft and light as a rose.
I smell the room, the sweet smell of the perfume.
The dust underneath me makes me sneeze.
I am made to make people comfy and warm.
My size is big and long as a limo.
My colour is white like a wedding dress.
I know how people feel once they are on me.

Gulsen Tosun (12)
Abington High School

Football

F antastic kicker
O ut of control
O ut of breath
T oo good for the players
B alls come up in the air
A ll people chant loud
L ots of people celebrating when we win
L ots of players swapping tops at the end.

Alex Nicholson (13)
Abington High School

My Life In The Cs

My caffeine is hot,
The capacity of the Caribbean.
I have a castle,
From a catalogue.
I have lots of calamities,
In my career as a cashier
I have my carriage
Which is in casualty.
I want a campaign,
A category of chaos.
My candidate is capable
Of ceasing a cough
And building a cathedral.
So, are you cautious
Of my character?
Which is not me
But maybe exists.

Clare Abbott (14)
Abington High School

Primary School

My primary school
Stays in my mind,
Fun and good times
Sun, rain or wind,
I wish I could do it again.

Remembering things I did
Trembling never mind,
I always had help on my side
My friends and staff were very kind,
I wish I could do it again.

I always used to act in plays
My place was to sing songs,
Presented with lots of marbles
Pretended to be Red Riding hood
Whilst on a foot pedal,
I wish I could do it again.

Aasiya Alana (16)
Ashfield School

What Is A Friend?

A friend is like a light
Shining through your heart,
Knowing that both of you
Shall never be apart.

A friend is like a lion
Who scares off all your troubles,
Arguments, fights
And even little squabbles.

A friend is like a blanket
Who is always there to cover you,
When you are distressed or lonely
You shall know you have someone to look up to.

A friend is like a maid
Who helps clean your life,
Without a friend
How will you survive?

Shazeena Majothi (12)
Crown Hills Community School

A Waste Of Life

My skin so silky and smooth
I have done nothing wrong
They're killing me for my skin to make products
I haven't been here very long.

I have no family
They've been killed too
There's no way anyone can stop them
There's nothing anyone can do.

These people batter us with clubs
I'm more than scared
Petrified is the word
Has anyone really cared?

They've killed me for their products
There's nothing in sight
Pray to God, I go to Heaven
And with my family I will reunite.

Zainab Adam (12)
Crown Hills Community School

Dragons

Dragons soaring through the air
Giving out a fiery blaze
Green and scaly with sharp teeth
In dark and gloomy caves.

Flying through the clouds
Standing on high mountains proud
Dragons are very loud
Dragons, dragons, dragons.

Ravi Maher (13)
Crown Hills Community School

Cricket

My hobby is cricket
It's a gentle game
In cricket you can
Swing, spin, slog, sweep, hook the ball.

There is an insect called a cricket
But my hobby cricket is different.
I like cricket better
Than any other sport.

The batsmen that's the best
Has to be Brian Lara
He made four-hundred runs
All by himself.

The bowler that's the best
Has to be Shoaib Akhtar
He's the fastest bowler in cricket
Cricket! My hobby is cricket.

Altamash Nazirahamed (12)
Crown Hills Community School

My Holiday

We went to Lanzarote.
We travelled on a plane.
The hotel was so beautiful.
We swam all day in the large cool pool.
We went on a boat - under the sea.
We ate ice cream - it was lovely!

Amy Vertigan (14)
Ellesmere College

Goldie

She liked to swim.
I liked my fish.
She lived in a tank.
I cleaned her bowl.
She blew bubbles.
I talked to my fish.

John Madgwick (14)
Ellesmere College

My Pet Dogs

They were my grandma's dogs
Toby chased sticks
Poppy is grey and black
They played tug of war
Poppy's alive but Toby has died.

They played in the park
They played tug of war
They barked at other dogs
Poppy's alive but Toby has died.

They made me feel good
I loved them a lot
They liked dog biscuits
Poppy's alive but Toby has died.

Hannah Khan (14)
Ellesmere College

My Grandma

My grandma was so beautiful.
She loved me very much.
She was cute like a baby with glasses on her nose.
She needed my help around the house.
She ate her biscuits mashed in tea.
She was so lovely.

Areefa Khan (14)
Ellesmere College

My Dog Purdy

She's funny.
She's a good dog.
I love my dog 'cause she protects our home!
I give her a walk to the park
So she can run around the field.
She's a good dog,
She's a very good dog
And I miss her so much when I'm at school.
I do love my dog!

Rebecca D'Souza (14)
Ellesmere College

The Other Side Of Truth
(Based on 'The Other Side Of Truth' by Beverly Naidoo)

Bang! The mother gets shot,
She falls into Sade's hands,
This was an awful plot.
Their father sends them to England,
Scared are Femi and Sade.

England, they are in,
In the dark, alone.
Will they find an inn?
Will they even find a bone?
Scared are Femi and Sade.

The police then take them in.
Femi and Sade then get questioned.
Soon they enter the house of the kings.
They had now learned
How scared were Femi and Sade.

Sade enters a school
Where she gets bullied.
They screw her work into a ball,
They then get to meet their father,
Now they weren't scared at all!

Conor Beattie (12)
English Martyrs School

I Am . . .

I am a weird boy that is obsessed with space.
I wonder what it is like at the end of the universe.
I hear buzzing of my fish tank filter throughout the night.
I see an alien on a faraway planet.
I want an adventure until the end of time.
I am a weird boy that is obsessed with space.

I pretend that I rule the world.
I feel the spin of our world at my feet.
I touch the grass, so green and sweet.
I worry about the end of the world.
I cry for all the people who have died.
I am a weird boy that is obsessed with space.

I understand that I cannot rule the world.
I say that this is for adults.
I dream of seeing the end of time.
I try to stay trying.
I hope that our beautiful world will never die.

I *am* a weird boy who is obsessed with space.

Matthew Walne (11)
English Martyrs School

I Am . . .

I am a crazy gal who likes shopping.
I wonder who invented high heeled shoes.
I hear my cat miaowing in the depths of the night.
I see the world as a better place.
I want to live for eternity.
I am a crazy gal who likes shopping.

I pretend that I rule over all the shops in the world.
I feel for the children dying in Africa.
I touch every shoe in the world.
I worry about the loss of my family in the future.
I cry for all the people getting murdered.
I am a crazy gal who likes shopping.

I understand that we aren't all perfect.
I say that children rule school.
I dream to see what I will look like in twenty years.
I try to succeed in everything I do.
I hope this world will be at peace at last.
I am a crazy gal who likes shopping.

Bernadette Woodley (11)
English Martyrs School

I Am . . .

I am a football-mad maniac who likes the colour red.
I wonder what I would be like when I am older.
I hear people around the world praying for peace.
I want there to be peace in the world and no wars.
I am a football-mad maniac who likes the colour red.

I pretend that sometimes I am another person.
I feel all the pain and joy around the world.
I touch and feel the air around me.
I worry about the future, what it would be like.
I cry about people's death and people's sadness.
I am a football-mad maniac who likes the colour red.

I understand that sometimes people cannot do anything
                                        to prevent wars.
I say that everyone deserves peace.
I dream that maybe someday I could help people.
I try to act as good as I can.
I hope that maybe one day, the enemy will realise how much pain
                                        they are causing.
I am a football-mad maniac who likes the colour red.

Gee-won Park (11)
English Martyrs School

I Am . . .

I am that girl that believes in angels.
I wonder if pigs can fly.
I hear the fizzing of my lemonade.
I see unicorns and ponies riding happily.
I would like to see the world from a different eye.
I am that girl who believes in angels.

I pretend to fly in my spare time.
I feel the prick of a thorn.
I touch the sky in a single bound.
I worry what could possibly go wrong.
I cry when I'm caught in a trap that I can't get out of.
I am that girl who believes in angels.

I understand what is wrong from right.
I speak what I really feel.
I dream for my wishes to all come true.
I try to make the most of my life.
I hope for when I can see my friends again.
I am that girl who believes in angels.

Melissa Law (12)
English Martyrs School

I Am . . .

I am a PlayStation 2, TV watching, playing maniac.
I wonder what the future is like.
I hear rockets in the air.
I see planes in the air.
I want a fluffy dog.
I am a PlayStation 2, TV watching, playing maniac.

I pretend to be the best in everything.
I feel a new game playing for school.
I touch the clouds in the air.
I worry about dying.
I cry after my last day at primary school.
I am a PlayStation 2, TV watching, playing maniac.

I understand the course that happens.
I say what should be said.
I dream of world peace.
I try to be good.
I hope everything will be OK in my life.
I am a PlayStation 2, TV watching, playing maniac.

Keanu Sherriff-Geary (11)
English Martyrs School

I Am . . .

I am a curious girl with a need to explore.
I wonder why people kill others in brutal ways.
I hear the voices of starving children crying for help.
I see an open world with millions of chances ahead of me.
I want to help others to stop people from dying of hunger or thirst.
I am a curious girl with a need to explore.

I pretend I'm the Prime Minister.
I feel the suffering of others in wars.
I touch the world and all its creations.
I worry about people who are in danger at this moment.
I cry for those with no hope.
I am a curious girl with a need to explore.

I understand anger and pain.
I say we're all important.
I dream of helping to make lives better.
I try to help my family at all times.
I hope wars will stop and that people will forgive.
I am a curious girl with a need to explore.

Suzanna Newton (11)
English Martyrs School

I Am . . .

I am a cheeky girl who is chocolate mad.
I wonder what it will be like to live on another planet.
I hear a camel trudging through the Sahara.
I see fish swimming in the Great Barrier Reef.
I want to travel this beautiful world.
I am a cheeky girl who is chocolate mad.

I pretend I am on a sunset beach.
I feel happy and jumping with joy.
I touch the white warm sand.
I worry what the world will be like in fifteen years.
I cry when people die in poverty.
I am a cheeky girl who is chocolate mad.

I understand that everything is fair.
I say we all have our own different ways.
I dream that poverty will stop.
I try my best in all my school work.
I hope cruelty will stop.
I am a cheeky girl who is chocolate mad.

Emily Gaskin (11)
English Martyrs School

I Am . . .

I am a sleepy person who likes to sleep.
I wonder why the sun comes out in the day.
I hear the stars twinkling.
I see the moon in the night.
I want to sleep all the time.
I am a sleepy person who likes to sleep.

I pretend that I am always asleep.
I feel the smoothness of the bed.
I touch the moon when I dream.
I worry when the sun comes out.
I cry when the sun comes up.
I am a sleepy person who likes to sleep.

I understand why there is light and dark.
I say I am always asleep.
I dream about travelling to the moon.
I try to reach the stars.
I hope I catch a star in the dark.
I am a sleepy person who likes to sleep.

Anu Joseph (11)
English Martyrs School

I Am . . .

I am a nutty girl who loves to gossip.
I wonder what I will be like in ten years' time.
I hear ghosts whispering as I try to get to sleep.
I see angels fluttering up in mid-air.
I want to be able to gallop off on my imaginative horse.
I am a nutty girl who loves to gossip.

I pretend that I am a millionaire taking over the world.
I feel the wind brisk against my face.
I touch out for the stars, the moon, the Earth.
I worry about the world coming to an end.
I cry for all the immigrants in this world.
I am a nutty girl who loves to gossip.

I say we are all even.
I dream of owning my own stables and learning to show jump.
I try to imagine that I am flying through space.
I hope to fulfil my dreams as I become older.
I am a nutty girl who loves to gossip.

Rebecca Fenn (12)
English Martyrs School

I Am . . .

I am a girl that loves cats and dogs.
I wonder how it feels on the moon.
I hear wars going on in the world.
I see people staring at me.
I want the world to be a better place.
I am a girl that loves cats and dogs.

I pretend that I can fly in the sky.
I feel like the world depends on me.
I touch the stars at night.
I worry about all the tests at school.
I cry for all the families that have recently lost a loved one.
I am a girl that loves cats and dogs.

I understand what is going on.
I say that we all have rights.
I dream about the clouds in the sky.
I try to be a good friend.
I hope that there will always be love in this world.
I am a girl that loves cats and dogs.

Emily Sherman (11)
English Martyrs School

I Am . . .

I am a mad footy fan with an Xbox.
I wonder who called dust, dust.
I hear the TV through my bedroom floor.
I see a goal scored by Gerrard or Bellamy.
I want to be the manager of Liverpool.
I am a mad footy fan with an Xbox.

I pretend I have not been to school after it's finished.
I feel my fingers moving every second.
I touch a pen in every lesson.
I worry about the homework my teacher might give me.
I cry when I think about my dad.
I am a mad footy fan with an Xbox.

I understand people have to be killed if it makes the world a
                                                better place.
I say we are all different people.
I dream of rooms that are fifteen miles long.
I try to create a new football skill.
I hope I'll be the new Steven Gerrard in ten years.
I am a mad footy fan with an Xbox.

Ben Shaw (11)
English Martyrs School

I Am . . .

I am a sporty girl who loves basketball.
I wonder what it would be like to enter a basketball studio.
I hear loudness coming from the crowds.
I see one of the basketball players scoring a goal.
I want the adventure to score that goal.
I am a sporty girl who loves basketball.

I pretend that I can be the best basketball player.
I feel that the world is going against me.
I touch the ball to score the highest.
I worry my friends won't cheer me when I score that goal.
I cry that one day I won't be the person I want to be.
I am a sporty girl who loves basketball.

I understand that some sport can be hard for some people.
I say that we are all the same.
I dream that one day I will get a trophy for the best basketball player.
I try to raise money for charity.
I hope that people won't take advantage of the poor.
I am a sporty girl who loves basketball.

Shylet Muza (11)
English Martyrs School

I Am . . .

I am a crazy boy who likes playing the drums.
I wonder what I will be like when I am older.
I hear seagulls screeching in the morning.
I see the stars shining bright.
I want to be famous.
I am a crazy boy who likes playing the drums!

I pretend that I am flying.
I feel the wind blowing my hair.
I touch the moon and stars.
I worry about my world.
I cry for the deaths in the world.
I am a crazy boy who likes playing the drums!

I understand I can't do everything.
I say everyone is different.
I dream of travelling the world.
I try to be a better person.
I hope peace will come to us on Earth.
I am a crazy boy who likes playing the drums!

Daniel Williamson (11)
English Martyrs School

I Am . . .

I am a beautiful boy who loves playing football.
I wonder when there will be no gravity on the world.
I hear people in the crowd shouting my name.
I see fit girls asking me out.
I want to play for Liverpool and England.
I am a beautiful boy who loves playing football.

I pretend that I've got the X Factor.
I feel like the world's on my shoulders.
I touch the green grass of Anfield.
I worry that the world will end in 2012.
I cry when an ant crawls on me.
I am a beautiful boy who loves playing football.

I understand that I can't score every game.
I say that I'm going to have kids.
I dream about being the best player in the world.
I try to be a good boy but it doesn't work.
I hope that Gerrard speaks to me.
I am a beautiful boy who loves playing football.

Aaron Gibbard (11)
English Martyrs School

I Am . . .

I am a sporty girl who loves netball.
I wonder how many feathers birds have.
I hear cats miaowing.
I see loads of goals being scored by me.
I want to live on a netball pitch.
I am a sporty girl who loves netball.

I pretend I am a professional netball player.
I feel the ball in my hands.
I touch my hair when it's been straightened.
I worry if we lose the game.
I cry when I fall or fail.
I am a sporty girl who loves netball.

I understand that we can't always win.
I say, 'Do the best you can!'
I dream that some day I will be a professional.
I try to get my hair as straight as possible.
I hope we get put through to the finals.
I am a sporty girl who loves netball.

Roberta Cooley (11)
English Martyrs School

I Am . . .

I am a fit guy who loves rugby.
I wonder how high the birds can fly.
I hear a wonderful crowd cheering my name.
I see lots of fit girls asking me out.
I want a place in the England rugby squad.
I am a fit guy who loves rugby.

I pretend I am on 'Top of the Pops' but I'm not.
I feel the crowd following me everywhere.
I touch the wet grass of a rugby pitch.
I worry about the end of the world when I will not see any girls.
I cry for all the girls that are never going to go out with me.
I am a fit guy who loves rugby.

I understand that not all the girls love me.
I say everyone can be like me.
I dream of getting married and having children.
I try so hard in rugby and everything I do
But there are always a couple of things I don't know.
I hope that I will be successful in my life.
I am a fit guy who loves rugby.

Aidan Fisher (11)
English Martyrs School

I Am . . .

I am a boy who likes maths and thinks it's easy.
I am a boy who can see the future.
I am a boy who can smell people from a mile off.
I am a boy who wonders what the meaning of life is.
I am a boy who likes maths and thinks it's easy.

Matthew Malone (11)
English Martyrs School

I Am . . .

I am a small girl who loves to dance.
I wonder when girls will be better than boys at everything.
I hear a loud beating sound at the crack of dawn.
I see bright pink stars in the sky.
I want to be small and tall at the same time.
I am a small girl who loves to dance.

I pretend to be the richest of them all.
I feel the happiness of the world lifting me up.
I touch the bubbly bouncy moon.
I worry about the poverty of the world.
I cry for all the people who don't survive operations.
I am a small girl who loves to dance.

I say we can all be winners.
I dream of travelling the whole world.
I try not to be ungrateful and disrespectful to the poor.
I hope the world will defeat the pollution and live longer.
I am a small girl who loves to dance.

Brenna Benjamin (11)
English Martyrs School

I Am . . .

I am a clever girl who loves netball.
I wonder what our world is going to be like in a million years.
I hear God speaking to me from Heaven.
I see angels watching over us.
I want to live in a world of peace with no poverty.
I am a clever girl who loves netball.

I pretend to fly over the world.
I feel the wars stopping and the people celebrating.
I touch the clouds.
I worry about what it is going to be like when the world does not exist.
I cry when I see countries fighting against each other
And people crying in pain and dying.
I am a clever girl who loves netball.

I understand that that's what life is like.
I say that we can make the world a better place.
I dream that I could be a singer and help poor countries.
I try to be the successful person in my life.
I hope that the world can improve
And that we can all try and make the world a better place.
I am a clever girl who loves netball.

Marlyce Pepe-Ngoma (11)
English Martyrs School

Spain

I've been to many places
A lot of them are the same
But I have to say my favourite place
Is definitely Spain.
Now Italy is great, USA is fine
But I must confess too much distress
My mum just loves the wine!
Portugal is cool and so is Turkey too
But in sunny Spain
There's just way more you can do.
Sweden was really great
Canada was fun,
But in great Spain you can't complain
About the shining sun.
Now Germany was great
France was a little cold,
But now I feel that sunny Spain
Is starting to get old!

George Muller (11)
English Martyrs School

Maths

Maths is cool
Maths is great
Maths is a piece of cake.

Bring a pen
Bring a pencil
Make sure you use a stencil.

Joshua Saunders (12)
English Martyrs School

I Am . . .

I am a computer freak who likes reading.
I wonder when someone will fly up to the sun.
I hear cats barking in the night.
I see computers in the air.
I want an adventure before I die.
I am a computer freak who likes reading.

I pretend I am an astronaut.
I feel other people's fears.
I see the sky, the stars, the moon and want to see the planets.
I worry about poverty.
I cry when an animal is killed.
I am a computer freak who likes reading.

I understand the frustration if you can't get something you want.
I say we are all different in our own way.
I dream I go on adventures inside the computer.
I hope the population will rise.
I try to reach out to the poor.
I am a computer freak who likes reading.

Gabrielle Flood (11)
English Martyrs School

I Am . . .

I am a timid boy who loves Arsenal FC.
I wonder if we will ever be able to go to other planets.
I see hip hop music in my head all day.
I see God welcoming me into Heaven.
I want to be a business man who will be the richest in the world.
I am a timid boy who loves Arsenal FC.

I pretend to be a hero who the world adores.
I feel like a hero.
I touch the World Cup when I beat Italy 7-0.
I worry about death and when it will strike next.
I cry when people verbally assault me.
I am a timid boy who loves Arsenal FC.

I understand that success comes with a price.
I say nothing is impossible if you put your mind to it.
I dream about time and when it will stop.
I try to succeed in everything I do.
I hope I will enjoy life with everything it brings me.
I am a timid boy who loves Arsenal FC.

Junior Manun'Ebo (11)
English Martyrs School

I Am . . .

I am a mad girl who likes to play football.
I wonder when dogs and cats will ever get on together.
I hear dogs miaowing.
I see the sun when it's rainy.
I want to be a crafty policewoman when I'm older.

I pretend I'm a professional footballer scoring one hundred goals.
I feel my school stuff each day.
I touch the World Cup trophy.
I worry about people who own Rottweilers.
I cry about people who are dying in horrible places.
I am a mad girl who likes football.

I understand there are rich people and poor people.
I say other people around the world are a bit greedy.
I dream when I'm older that I will save people's lives.
I hope when I'm older people will not fight,
Enjoy living in a non-poverty part of the world and think about people
                                                                    who are poor.
I am a mad girl who likes to play football.

Chloe Randall (12)
English Martyrs School

I Am A Funny Lad

I am a funny lad who loves football.
I wonder what football will be like in many years to come.
I hear football commentators at midnight.
I see the world's best footy player giving his autograph to me.
I want to be a professional football player.
I am a funny lad who loves football.

I pretend I am a drag racer.
I feel life goes on forever.
I touch the World Cup for England.
I worry poverty won't end.
I cry when people I love or admire pass away.
I am a funny lad who loves football.

I understand everything happens for a reason.
I say Jesus is the Light of the World.
I dream what life will be like one thousand years from today.
I try my hardest in all ambitions.
I hope worldwide, no one will suffer.
I am a funny lad who loves football.

Connell Smyth (11)
English Martyrs School

I Am . . .

I am an ecstatic guy who loves aeroplanes.
I wonder when the public will be able to have holidays on Mars.
I hear cows barking.
I see pigs flying.
I want to travel the world.
I am an ecstatic guy who loves aeroplanes.

I pretend I am a millionaire.
I feel full of life.
I touch the surface of Mars.
I worry about global warming.
I cry when animals' habitats are destroyed.
I am an ecstatic guy who loves aeroplanes.

I understand I will not live forever.
I say live life to the full.
I dream of being a pilot.
I try to study hard and learn the aspects involved in being a pilot.
I am an ecstatic guy who loves aeroplanes.

Jack Snart (11)
English Martyrs School

I Am . . .

I am a cool dude who loves football.
I wonder when the aliens are going to live with mankind.
I hear fishes saying, 'Fishy nibbles,' and barking.
I see a lion break-dancing.
I want to ride around the world in eighty days.
I am a cool dude who loves football.
I pretend to become a huge carrot.
I feel animals' fur around my chest.
I touch the sun in the sky barehanded.
I worry about the Earth.
I cry for the people who have died.
I am a cool dude who loves football.
I understand if you are good you go to Heaven.
I say I believe in the future.
I dream of being the richest man on Earth.
I try not to get myself told off.

Christian Kamara (11)
English Martyrs School

I Am . . .

I am a girl who bruises easily and likes swimming.
I wonder what I will be when I'm older.
I hear the sound of the sea rushing against the rocks.
I see myself when I'm grown up.
I want to be an Olympic swimmer when I am an adult.
I am a girl who bruises easily and likes swimming.
I pretend I am the best swimmer.
I feel my dog's fur when I'm sleeping.
I touch my duvet in my sleep when I'm dreaming.
I worry about my uncle that he will die of cancer.
I cry when I don't feel very well.
I am a girl who bruises easily and likes swimming.
I understand what happens when you die.
I say God is real.
I dream I will have a good life.
I try to make my life easy.
I hope the wars will stop.
I am a girl who bruises easily and likes swimming.

Amy Day (11)
English Martyrs School

I Am . . .

I am a strange boy who loves computers but I am popular.
I wonder how long it will be until children can stand on the moon.
I hear whales screeching.
I see myself being knighted by the Queen.
I want to find my best talent to be the best.
I am a strange boy who loves computers but I am popular.

I pretend I am invincible.
I feel someone's life on my shoulders.
I touch sharks, whales and dolphins.
I worry about the end of the world.
I cry about the poverty and the anger in the world.
I am a strange boy who loves computers but I am popular.

I understand how our money can change someone's life.
I say when you are clear you are ready to go.
I dream about the next day and how I make it better.
I try to do my best in everything I do.
I hope all the poverty will stop.
I am a strange boy who loves computers but I am popular.

Thomas Lloyd-Jones (12)
English Martyrs School

Animals Are . . .

Animals are funny
Some swing on trees and eat bananas
While others will swim and eat salmon.
Animals are silly
They can't speak, read or write
They can't wear clothes or shoes.
Animals are superstars
Some sing a song or a lullaby
Some screech in envy
But most of all may I ask
What are animals for?

Abigail Leader (11)
English Martyrs School

The Girl In The Library

In the library she's always there,
Chewing her nails or sucking her hair.
Ever since I saw her she's been on page five
Barely awake, or even alive.

All she does is sit and stare,
Not moving a muscle and hardly aware.
All her focus is on the page,
With no sign of sadness, no sign of rage.

How she does it, I do not know,
Going so calmly, being so slow.
Her hair flops in front of her face,
As she sets her steady pace.

A deep shade of blue are her eyes,
But they lack emotion, lack surprise.
Ring! Ring! There goes the bell,
She carries on reading as I bid farewell!

Olivia Norris (12)
English Martyrs School

My Family Are . . .

My family are . . .
People to look after me
A place I'm always welcome
People to run to
A place I know I will be safe
A mad roller coaster
A fantastic, loud CD
A funny clown
A cute kitten
A feisty dinosaur
A wish made come true
A genie in a bottle
A mission impossible
A laugh to the world
A sweet strawberry
A joke machine
A place like no other.

Abigail Kearney (11)
English Martyrs School

The Sea

The sea is . . .
A sheet of blue
A giant pool
A snorkler's paradise
An underwater home
A world of fish
A fisherman's kitchen
A torrent of water
A flooded beach
A dangerous place
A flow of tears
A frozen land
A penguin's ice rink
An explorer's quest
A polar bear's kingdom.

George Richards (11)
English Martyrs School

The Best Of Friends

My friends are . . .
Comfortable chairs,
Delicious chocolate,
Hip hop feet
And crazy cats.
Big huggable bears,
A long swishing tail,
Big blankets of wool
And high heel stilettos.
Warm cosy fire,
Blooming daffodils,
Glittering gloss
And large juicy fruits.
The crackle of sparkles,
Adventurous dreams,
An open window
And a gleaming diamond ring.
Soft pillows,
Laughing lions
And most of all fantastic friends.

Emily White (11)
English Martyrs School

Football Is . . .

Football is . . .
A match made in Heaven.
The darkest part of Hell.
A huge dragon.
The fiercest battle.
A heart grasping challenge.
A lion's roar.
A racing heartbeat.
A broken heart.
A flying saucer whizzing through the air.
A ticking time bomb.
A speeding missile.
A spitting cobra.
A raging war.
A young cheetah.

Robert Law (11)
English Martyrs School

Dancing Is Like . . .

Dancing is like . . .
Wind rushing through leaves.
Rain tapping on a glass window.
A child's peak of laughter.
The sun beaming down on the Earth.
The joy of a newborn baby's parents.
The feeling of winning a gold medal.
Like winning the lottery.
Your first kiss.
Meeting your favourite celebrity.
Like the breeze running through your hair.
The sound of the sea.
The smile of a little baby.

Rhianna Stretton (11)
English Martyrs School

A Good Friend Is . . .

A good friend is . . .
A guardian angel.
A shoulder to cry on.
A brave lion standing up to people.
A big hugging machine.
A blanket warm and cuddly.
A good day out (fun and exciting).
A firework keeping its spark.
A parrot on your shoulder.
A cash machine.
Your own fashion expert.
A life-sized teddy bear.
The gentle sea.
A person with the world at their feet.
A dictionary of tips.
An extra pair of hands.

Charlotte Richardson (11)
English Martyrs School

Fire Is . . .

Fire is . . .
A warm sensation rushing through the body,
An angry shout from a fierce dragon's mouth,
Dancing, twirling in the mysterious glaze,
The sizzling sound of grilling bacon,
Light, set into the sky,
A glow reflected on people's rosy faces,
Joyful songs sang around the blaze,
A large blinding light,
Millions of miles away, the bright dot in the sky,
High, low, big, small, all dancing happily, vastly spreading,
In the darkened night, the sky was set a light by a giant ball of fire,
Beautifully blending with the scarlet eyes of magical creatures,
Yellow, orange and red ribbon blowing in the wind,
Roasting, crisp and dull, burning hot ash,
Dangerous explosions - like sausages popping in the pan.

Joanna Uczniak (11)
English Martyrs School

Football Is . . .

Football is . . .
The grass is green,
The grass is cut and painted,
The fans are seated,
The players appear,
The whistle goes,
The players run,
The managers shout,
The defence protects their goal,
The midfielders battle,
The strikers score,
The fans cheer,
The players urge each other,
The strikers shoot,
The keeper saves,
The player is fouled,
The fans protest,
It's a . . .
Penalty!
The striker hits it . . .
Goal!
Game over
We won!

Connor Wickwar (11)
English Martyrs School

The Sky Is . . .

The sky is . . .
Twinkling diamonds shimmering above your head,
A painting with clouds dabbed in,
A blue velvet sheet hugging the clouds,
The world separated in two.

A massive shiny ball of topaz,
The beginning of the Earth,
A giant electrical voltage ball,
Something that keeps you warm when the sun is shining,
Glowing with happiness and joy.

Irritating when the clouds go dark,
A Bunsen burner on its hottest flame,
Blue wallpaper wrapped around the world,
Something to stare at when you are bored,
The raving blue seas.

James Fernandez-Harrison (11)
English Martyrs School

Music Is . . .

Music is . . .
An ear's paradise,
A sea of notes,
A babbling brook,
A language nobody has ever spoken,
A story waiting to be discovered,
Black ink,
A spring morning,
Wind through bamboo sticks,
Birds singing,
A thunderstorm on a winter's night,
Rain on a windowpane,
Children playing at break time,
Wine glasses chinking in celebration,
A baby's first cry,
A clock ticking,
Traffic noise,
The *slosh, slosh, slosh* of a washing machine,
Lips kissing,
Dogs barking,
Cooks in a kitchen,
Potatoes bubbling in a pan,
Popcorn popping.

Jak Skelly (11)
English Martyrs School

The Jungle Is . . .

The jungle is . . .
An elephant's stampede,
An ant's worst nightmare,
A monkey's kingdom,
A bird's song,
A spider's home,
The wind's howl,
A gorilla's paradise,
A tribe's place to live,
A tree's luxury,
A snake's misfortune
And the rain's happiness.
Also, a worm's territory,
The sun's comfort,
The leaves without any sunlight
And a deadly poison machine.

Charlotte Waite (11)
English Martyrs School

Basketball Is . . .

Basketball is . . .
Iverson's restaurant,
Karl Brown's garden,
A work machine,
A street game,
It's like holding a rock,
O'Neill's runway,
It's a player's delight,
Only for kings,
Not for the weak,
Happy people,
Cheering sides,
A team of hard-working men,
It is a hand from the sky,
A place for respect.

Lydon D'Costa (11)
English Martyrs School

The Other Side Of Truth
(Inspired by 'The Other Side Of Truth' by Beverly Naidoo)

I have lost my father and my mother,
Is there any other?
Is there any hope?
I've not even enough energy to mope!
My mother was killed in a drastic way,
Those gunmen shall soon have to pay.
They hurt me deep inside,
They can run but they can't hide.
I don't know why it was me,
Nobody can see.
I have restless nights,
Where I came from was just pain and fright.
At school I get picked on for who I am.
Later one night I had a dream,
My mother's death was a scam,
It was my father's fault.
I wish I could seal all of the dreadful past away,
But I know that it's here to stay.

Hannah O'Neill (12)
English Martyrs School

The Other Side Of The Truth
(Inspired by 'The Other Side of Truth' by Beverly Naidoo)

Bang! Bang! Bang!
Poor Mama was dead
She lay before Papa and painfully bled
A zooming car went screeching down the road and fled.

Ring! Ring! Ring! A noisy phone rang
Sade picked it up and a scary man sang,
'I will kill you first and then I'll kill your dad
You're so stupid and I'm so bad!'

Vroom! Vroom! Vroom! The crazy plane flew
Across the hills while people ate stew.
After landing they couldn't find shelter
So they went to stay with a social worker.

Ew! Ew! Ew! She's from Jamaica
She's even got a new paper stapler,
Ha! Ha! Ha! Poor Sade got bullied
Never noticing her homework needs to get studied.

Joseph Stoneleigh (12)
English Martyrs School

The Other Side Of Truth
(Inspired by 'The Other Side of Truth' by Beverly Naidoo)

The two gunshots and the piercing cry of Papa
Sent a shiver down Sade's spine
And a million thoughts ran through her mind.

Nothing can get the thought of Mama being taken away
Under the bloodstained cloth and the screeching
Sound of the tyres as they drove away.

The threatening words from the stranger on the other line
Then the conversation that Papa and Uncle Dele had
About having Sade and Femi sent to England.

One hour, that is all they had to pick from so many things
That remind them of Mama
How would they know what to do after the trauma of losing
                                                                                                their mother?

A kind-looking face enters the room
Only to tell Sade and Femi that this is the woman that will take
                                                                                                them to England
And will have to act like their mother until they are in England.

They arrive and the bag that Sade had brought was tugged at
                                                                                      and ripped into shreds
Sade's heart sank, then to find out that the only person that could
                                                                                help wasn't there.

Soon after the Kings had started to foster the two troubled children
And had to get them started at school
When they told Sade the words ringing in her head
What was she meant to do?

Sade was having a hard time at school from the bully of 8M
When the women from the foster agency said she needed
                                                                                 to talk to them
Their faces turned to ice in fear of what she might have to tell them.

To their surprise it was good news
She had come to tell them that their father had made it to England
But couldn't be with them because he was in jail!

Keira Wall (13)
English Martyrs School

I Try Not To Cry
(Based on 'The Other Side of Truth' by Beverly Naidoo)

A bang, a scream, a shout,
Tyres screeching on the road that is dry
Mama lying in the drive
I try not to cry.

Me and my brother have to leave
Because Papa doesn't lie
We want Papa now
I try not to cry.

We're on the plane with a stranger
We couldn't say goodbye
We're so terrified
I try not to cry.

We're in England
The stranger meets this guy
Then they disappear
I try not to cry.

We go into a shop
Then thugs come in very sly
They smash everything up
I try not to cry.

The police rush in
And stare into my eye
They take us away
I try not to cry.

We're put in a room all alone
A man comes in and asks why
He takes us away
I try not to cry.

We go to one house
My brother starts to cry
We move to another
I try not to cry.

We go to a new school
I'll give it a try
Some girls are not nice
I try not to cry.

We find Papa
He had to lie
So we could be happy
Now I can cry!

Tasmin Kennedy (12)
English Martyrs School

The Other Side Of Truth
(Based on 'The Other Side of Truth' by Beverly Naidoo)

Noise. Fear. Blood. Shock.
The phone rings, an evil voice that threatens,
'Even children are not safe'
Because my father speaks.

His newspaper prints his words
They do not like his words
Truth is a crime here
Punishable by death.

Father, brother and me
Alone against the world
A whirl of activity as we fly from danger
But Father stays behind; will we ever see him again?

New country, strange ways.
Woman we should trust betrays.
Abandoned, terrified, without knowing why.
Searching for an uncle who is all we have.

Surrounded by people who treat us like lepers,
At last this is where our uncle should be, but he is missing.
Dear Lord, does it reach here too?
No money. No home.

We join the ranks of the homeless on the street.
Noses pressed against the glass.
We cannot buy
Into a shop, selling film and food, we enter only for warmth.

Witness robbery, we are blamed.
Police! Do we fear or do we trust?
Moved here and there to foster homes.
At last the Immigration Office says we are legal.

Sent to school where bullies threaten. Everywhere the same.
Is this the world?
Forced to steal against my will. Betray the only friend I have.
I shall regret this all my life.

Finally, joyful news.
Our father is in this country.
In detention true,
But now we may hope.

Fern Watkins (12)
English Martyrs School

The Other Side Of The Truth
(Based on 'The Other Side Of Truth' by Beverly Naidoo)

My name is Sade, I am but twelve
I am from Nigeria but now in London
My mama is dead, what a drama life has been
From country to country, family to family
Not knowing where we would be.

From Mrs Appiah to Mr and Mrs King
What help they have been to get us through
Papa at home and Uncle Dele missing
We have tried to call, where have they been?

My horrors of England have all come true
School is a nightmare with nobody to talk to
Marcia is a bully, what will she make me do?
I just wish I had someone to turn to.

What great news, we have heard finally
Papa has made his way here,
But the overwhelming sadness hits again
Papa has ended himself in jail
How will this life in England ever end?

Gabrielle Parkinson (12)
English Martyrs School

The Other Side Of Truth
(Based on 'The Other Side Of Truth' by Beverly Naidoo)

Bang! Bang!
Two shots only
Ran outside, my mama was shot
I got a threatening phone call
I must get away.

Met Mrs Bankhole
Nice she seemed
Got smuggled out of the country
Arrived in England for the very first time
We must get away.

Wandered around London alone
Mrs Bankhole left us
We were alone
Found no one, not even our uncle
I must get away.

Near dark
Police found us and took us
Stayed with Mrs Graham
Who was our foster parent
We must get away.

Stayed with Mr and Mrs King
Went to school
Hate it here
Being bullied by Marcia
I must get away.

Good news has come
Father was in England
But in jail!
What will happen to us?
We must get away.

Gee-Young Park (12)
English Martyrs School

The Other Side Of Truth
(Based on 'The Other Side Of Truth' by Beverly Naidoo)

One shot, two shots, silence
I rush down to the veranda
I see nothing but a still body
The still body being my mother
Surrounded by deep red thick blood.

Father kneeling beside her
Broken down in tears
My heart splits in two
My head spinning
Why did it have to be Mother?

A quick escape to London
Where we might be safe
But where to go the question still remains
We're put in care where Mrs Graham takes us in
Where's Father?

Mrs Graham is very nice
She has a son and twins
Her son is not that pleasant
I know he doesn't like me and Femi very much
But we don't stay there for long.

We get moved to the King's house
Their children are all grown up
We are put in schools
But I don't fit in that well
I get bullied and teased with my name.

They find my father
He's in a prison
He doesn't look the same
Will he ever be the same again?
Will we ever be safe?

Olivia Cluskey (12)
English Martyrs School

The Other Side Of Truth
(Based on 'The Other Side Of Truth' by Beverly Naidoo)

My name is Sade
I am twelve years old
I lived in Nigeria
Until things went wrong.

My mother got shot
My uncle disappeared
My father's in danger
And I live with a stranger.

I'm sad and lonely
My father's in jail
My brother won't speak to me
I'm getting bullied at school.

My dad's in jail
My mother is now dead
My uncle has gone
What more can go wrong?

Laura McLoughlin (12)
English Martyrs School

The Other Side Of The Truth
(Based on 'The Other Side Of Truth' by Beverly Naidoo)

It is so sad our mum has died
It is so sad we won't see her again
It is so sad we must leave Nigeria
It is so sad we must leave our home.

It is so strange travelling to England
It is so strange Mrs Bankhole has abandoned us
It is so strange Uncle Dele is missing
It is so strange this new country.

It is so lonely walking around London
It is so lonely although there are so many people
It is so lonely we have been mugged
It is so lonely, we have been trapped.

It is not fair our mum is not here
It is not fair we live in this house we don't know
It is not fair our dad's been arrested
It is not fair we can't see our parents.

Jacob Brown (12)
English Martyrs School

The Other Side Of Truth
(Based on 'The Other Side Of Truth' by Beverly Naidoo)

Sade and Femi, what a life they have
Their father writes truth for his newspaper
The Nigerian government tells lies
And they don't go together!

Sade and Femi, what a life they have
Their mum has been shot
So they get smuggled to London
And they are lost here.

Sade and Femi, what a life they have
Darth Vader of the alley taking what they have
Social services taking them in
Putting them with Mrs Graham and moaning Kevin.

Sade and Femi, what a life they have
Sade is being bullied by Marcia
And doesn't know what to do
She has so much troubling her, does she need more?

Sade and Femi, what a life they have
United with their father at last
Talking to Mr Seven O'clock news
And all the efforts seem to have paid off.

Daniel Leung (12)
English Martyrs School

I Am . . .

I am an animal loving, dancing diva.
I wonder when the world will end.
I hear the sound of birds and the breeze through the trees.
I see the sky full of beautiful angels.
I want to help animals and people around the world.
I am an animal loving, dancing diva.

I pretend I am better than everybody else.
I feel the feelings that nobody else does.
I touch the things that are impossible to touch.
I worry about my future and not reaching my dream.
I cry for the people who lose their homes and family in disasters.
I am an animal loving, dancing diva.

I understand the feeling of losing somebody or something close to you.
I say everybody is different but all equal.
I dream of travelling the world.
I try to be the same as everybody else.
I hope I am as good as everybody else.
I am an animal loving, dancing diva.

Vienna Bradley (11)
English Martyrs School

I Am . . .

I am a funky girl who loves dogs.
I wonder what the world will look like in the year 2080.
I hear the sound of dogs calling my name.
I see ants making world domination.
I want to be able to fly.
I am a funky girl who loves dogs.

I pretend I am on stage performing worldwide.
I feel the weight of all the planets on my shoulders.
I touch the sky with my head when I'm happy.
I worry about people not surviving operations.
I cry when people of the world die.
I am a funky girl who loves dogs.

I understand that nobody can live forever.
I say there are no mistakes.
I dream of world peace.
I hope that I achieve well in the world.
I am a funky girl who loves dogs.

Jessica Dawson (11)
English Martyrs School

The Other Side Of Truth
(Based on 'The Other Side Of Truth' by Beverly Naidoo)

When Sade's mum gets shot
Sade gets a big shock
Because she has to leave her papa
To go to her uncle Dele.

When they get there
They get left alone,
And Uncle Dele's missing
They meet Darth Vader of the valley.

They get arrested
And go to a temporary care home
And find a boy that hates them
They leave the next day
And find a loving home.

They also find their papa
Who also gets arrested
They leave their papa lone
And they go home.

Daniel Desewu (12)
English Martyrs School

Poems

Poems are for writing things
That let you float away.
You can write them about the siege of Troy
Or a well planned foray

           You   can

                 Make

          Them   into

               Shapes

    Or write
   them in the
    middle.
Poems are for writing things
That let you float away.
You can write a lot of nonsense words
To brighten up your day.

Poems, poems, poems, I love all kinds
They bring pleasure to all sorts of minds.

Matthew Gilmore (12)
Garendon High School

The Daily Trudge

I leave the warmth of home for the cold and wet.
My back weighed down by my heavy bag of books.
Thoughts of school and homework flit through my brain.
My feet drag slowly to the sweet shop where my friends stand waiting.
The wind spins leaves in the air
The rain continues to batter my raincoat.
We trudge through muddy patches of dirt.
Up the hill, down the hill and through the familiar archway.
Cars whizz by as we wait for the green man to appear.
One last climb, finally, I'm out of the weather,
Oh no! I'm at school!

Josh Nicholls (12)
Garendon High School

Whispers

Whispers, whispers,
As soft as a mouse,
Not letting anyone stir in the house.

Whispers, whispers,
Midnight chats,
Sweets and chocolates hidden in hats.

Whispers, whispers,
Pretending to sleep,
Laughing and giggling until you weep.

Whispers, whispers,
With a friend
Hoping the night will never end.

Jessica Thorpe (12)
Garendon High School

Mr Meaner

Our teacher Mr Meaner
Is no cleaner
Than the school dustbin.

His hair is fluffy
His shoes are scruffy
And certainly belong in a skip.

His hands are black
His teeth have plaque
His clothes belong in a sack.

He needs a shower
To smell like a flower
He needs it this very hour.

His face is scabby
His belly is flabby
He needs to go to the gym.

A bath he finds frightening
Like it could get struck by lightning
And that would be the end of him.

Dominic Cunliffe (12)
Garendon High School

Hallowe'en

Spooky, scary, dark,
Bats flying in the park
Children eating sweets
Ghosts made of sheets.

Pumpkin candles flicker
The night is cold and bitter,
A frosty cover on the floor
Witches knocking on a door.

Trick or treat? Trick or treat?
Echoing around the street,
A young boy dressed as Dracula
Another Hallowe'en spectacular.

Hannah Johnston (12)
Garendon High School

Autumn

It is autumn, the leaves are golden.
It is autumn, the leaves are falling.
It is autumn, the conkers are ripe.
It is autumn, the conkers are falling.
It is autumn, it's getting dark.
It is autumn, it's getting cold.

Josh Platts (12)
Garendon High School

Precious Times Of Love

I knew as soon as I met you
My dreams could come true.
I found such a wonderful man
Deep inside of you.

You know I love you deeply
More than words can say.
I love you more and more
With every passing day.

When you kiss me in the morning
And hold me close at night.
I have never felt so happy
Until you came into my life.

We will be together forever
Until time decides that we should part.
But you will stay with me forever
Right here in my heart.

Lauren O'Connell (12)
Garendon High School

What Am I?

Strolling through the forest,
Hunting for prey,
Hunting at night,
Asleep mostly at day.

Mysteriously spying,
Waiting to pounce,
Slashing at the meat
What a trounce!

Hiding in the shadows,
Looking for some dinner,
A deer trots by,
What a winner!

Orange and black,
Flashes past,
Visible colour,
Chasing after animals, running fast!

Stephanie Willis (12)
Garendon High School

The Fair

The huge big wheel,
The scary rides,
The people screaming,
Loud music thudding,
The hot dogs cooking,
Sticky toffee apples,
The cold ride bars,
The fluffy candyfloss,
The smell of sweets all over town,
I feel free.

Michael Meyerstein (12)
Garendon High School

My Family

We love each other very much
We are very close
If I saw a gorgeous flower
I would call it a rose!

My family is special to me
Everywhere I go,
Whatever I make
I always love to show.

Sometimes they make me laugh
If I do something funny,
And if they say my name
They might call me Bunny.

I bring something for my family
Everywhere I go,
And then get them a sunflower
To make them glow!

Tejal Patel (12)
Garendon High School

Someone Once Told Me

Someone once told me
There is a place where bunnies are purple and eat popcorn.

Someone once told me
There is a place where blue trees go out partying every Saturday night.

Someone once told me
There is a place where the grass is pink and the sky is green.

Someone once told me
There is a place where orange elephants drive around in Minis.

Someone once told me
There is a place where yellow carrots rule the lands.

Someone once told me
There is a place where little kids believe everything that is said . . .
I wonder where it is?

Calum Kirk (11)
Garendon High School

Brothers!

Aren't they annoying?
Those nasty stinking brothers,
Always in your way,
Tugging one way or another.

Aren't they horrible?
Them nasty little bros,
Never brushing their hair
Always picking their nose.

Don't they just bug you?
Right throughout the day,
Making me wonder
If he'd just go away.

Now that he's gone
It's getting really dim,
His bedroom's empty,
And I actually miss him!

Charlotte Jones (11)
Garendon High School

Here Comes Christmas

C hristmas is coming, snow's everywhere
H ats, scarves and gloves, in the cold winter air.
R olling up snowballs and out on my sledge
I t's getting close now, I'm all on edge!
S o excited I really can't sleep
T rees full of presents, I can't help but peep
M um wasn't happy
A nd then she said,
'S anta's not coming, he's staying in bed!'

Alex Thomas (11)
Garendon High School

Dreams

There are lots of different types of dreams,
Bad dreams,
Good dreams,
Scary dreams,
Happy dreams.

Dreams that make you wake with fear
Then you lie awake hoping that it won't carry on,
There are also dreams that are really good
And you wake up just as they're getting to the best bit.

Sometimes dreams make you believe that they actually happened
And you have to ask someone just to make sure.

Sometimes dreams make you jolt
As if you have just fallen down a great big bottomless pit
And you wake up to find yourself not in a great big bottomless pit,
But a cosy, warm bed wrapped up in a duvet.

But the dreams that I like best of all
Are the ones that let you have a really good night's sleep.

Lydia Brown (13)
Garendon High School

Why Do Boys Smell?

Why do boys smell?
Why are boys weird?
Why do they pick their noses
And pick earwax out of their ears?

Why are they always dirty?
Why do they never wash?
They could try using deodorant,
It won't turn them posh.

Why are boys annoying?
Always pulling faces.
Do they have no manners?
Those sweaty hairy disgraces.

Why are boys so silly?
Why are they so mean?
I hate them so much,
They make me want to scream!

Megan McTavish (11)
Garendon High School

What Am I?

Long neck
Quick runner
Very stable
Sharp teeth
More than one colour
Leaf eater
Short legs
Brown spots
Not found in England
Apart from zoos.
I ask again
What am I?

Matthew Bassett (11)
Garendon High School

My Pet Ladybird

My pet ladybird died yesterday
I took it to the swimming pool
And it drowned straight away!

My pet bluebottle flew away yesterday
I took it out fishing
And it quickly sped away!

My parents went to the pet shop yesterday,
They bought me a snail,
Which slowly slipped away!

My advice is to never have a pet
Because mine . . .
. . . Didn't like me!

Megan Bass (11)
Garendon High School

Percy Penguin

Percy Penguin's a very bad boy,
He swam away
And came back with a toy.
Stolen it was,
And then he got more.
He stole from the rich
And he stole from the poor!

Greedy he was, the shameful bird,
He didn't care,
But how absurd.
By doing this,
To jail he'll go,
Then he will be
Full of woe!

So stop, Percy, don't be so bad.
By doing this,
It will drive your mum mad!
She'll go insane,
Because of you,
So steal no more
And do something new.

He listened to me and off he went,
Undoing the wrong he had done.
He returned the toys, became a real gent,
Being kind to everyone!

Samantha Tyler (11)
Garendon High School

Fog On The Way To School

The fog on the way to school
Is a magical curtain of fluff.
The trees stick out oddly
I push my hands further into my cuffs.

The end of the street is hidden
All I can see is a pair of lights,
As a car cruises down the road
It disappears down the road to the right.

It makes my head feel damp and cold
I'm glad I have a big fluffy coat
My fingers are white and frozen
But I feel like singing at the back of my throat.

I feel all happy and tingling
Because I know that warmth is near,
And also because it feels like
Christmas will soon be here.

Elizabeth Callan (12)
Garendon High School

In The Land Where Trees Are Purple

In the land where trees are purple
And the sky is green,
Marshmallows are rock hard
And bunny rabbits are mean.

In the land where trees are purple
And the sky is green,
Monkeys eat grass
And cows eat beans.

In the land where trees are purple
And the sky is green,
Coffee beans run around
And oranges are lean.

In the land where trees are purple
And the sky is green,
Anything can happen
After all, it is my imagination!

Christopher Mitchell (11)
Garendon High School

A Typical Morning

Eight o'clock get up, get out of bed,
I feel like a car ran over my head.
Skip breakfast because I've got to go
Haven't got any time to take it slow.

Oh no, my hair is in a mess
And I haven't yet got dressed.
Just another day of stress and sorrow,
And I will do my hair tomorrow!

Oh no, I've spilt my cup of tea,
This day cannot get any worse for me.
No time to take it slow,
Because I'm always on the go!

Callum Bowley (11)
Garendon High School

Autumn Thoughts

A nimals ready to hibernate
U nique season of colours
T umbling leaves rustling under footsteps
U p in the sky, fireworks blaze
M ist covers the ground
N oel is coming!

Abigail Lee (11)
Garendon High School

Spain

Swimming pools full of children playing
The sea rushing and splashing
Planes buzzing
The golden sand
The fresh air
Food as it is made
The wind brushing on my cheeks
I feel alive!

Ashton Allen (11)
Garendon High School

The Middle Of The Fair!

People of all sizes running through the crowd,
Big, fast and scary rides racing through the night air,
Loud music coming from all directions,
People chatting about all things possible,
Hot dogs sizzling and some burning,
The rides burning precious fuel
The taste of sizzling hot dogs raced through the cold air,
The loud music running through my body
The fantastic feeling has now come!

Emma Wright (11)
Garendon High School

Egypt

The Sphinx towering over everyone else
The pyramids for real life
Camels making a disgusting noise
People talking on open top tour buses
Camels stink with flies smothering them
Sand, the breeze brushes it up in my face
Amazed is the feeling I get from Egypt.

Will Roe (11)
Garendon High School

Seaside

Pretty sandcastles
Squawking seagulls
Gently lapping waves
Happy families
Salty sea
Glorious packed lunch
Chocolate ice cream
Gentle breeze
Soft sand
I can't wait to get going.

Louise Cox (11)
Garendon High School

Pizza Hut

Round, big, juicy pizzas
Manky brown salad and cold pasta
People smacking their lips together
Freezing cold Coke
Cheesy pizzas with lots of toppings
Cheese, tomato, pineapple, pepperoni, peppers
I feel sick!

Laith Al-Samawi (11)
Garendon High School

Winter

Summer was here
Now it has gone
Time to get your gloves and scarves on
Wait for snow and when it comes
Mess around with your friends
Later on comes Christmas
A happy holiday, Christmas trees and lots of joy
I think the best season is winter.

Giorgia Francis (12)
Garendon High School

Last Chance

Oh my word, this is such a bore
But wait, our player's got the ball!
He puts it through a player's legs
And magically the whole stadium, shouts, 'Megs!'
He puts a cross in from the side
'Head it,' I hear our crowd cry.
Our player roars into the box, heads it . . .
Oh my word, how did he miss?

Tomasz Williams (12)
Garendon High School

People

People can be crazy
They can be weird,
We make different decisions!
Large people,
Skinny people,
We make different decisions!
Long hair,
Short hair,
We make different decisions!
Soft skin,
Rough skin,
We make different decisions!
Hair up,
Hair down,
We make different decisions!
Tall
And small,
We are all different!

Sarah Blanchard (11)
Garendon High School

The Dark Valley

Green hills overlap, I wonder what lurks behind.
Faces in the blue sky whispering to me.
The birds sign in discomfort.
The natural fresh air goes in my lungs feeling like poison.
The trees swaying are going to grab me, what can I do?

Mayank Patel (11)
Garendon High School

The Colourful World

A huge colourful backyard wall but very far away
A long and very dark green hedge that is very near
A blue river going down stream that I can hear
The strong wind rustles in trees
While the rain splashing everywhere even on my knees
The short and especially green grass growing like a jungle
The beautiful chicken in the oven of heat
The multicoloured flowers that my brother will eat.

Darren Smith (11)
Garendon High School

Antarctica

Black and white fat penguins
Running in the snow
I can hear loud noises
Coming from the bears
A polar bear chasing after seals
I can smell nothing but dead fish.

Krishan Patel (11)
Garendon High School

The Cruise

The dark blue ocean moving slowly
The shiny white cruise ship going up and down
The waves crashing against the ship
The wind whistling in my ear
The wind blowing against me
The pure water in my mouth
The burger on my tongue
The barbecue smoking up in the air
The salty sea splashing up.

Thomas Skillen (11)
Garendon High School

The Swamp Of Demons

Cold mist and wet weeds.
I can hear frogs and the creepy water moving.
I can smell a dark cloud of a horrible smell of dead frogs!
Dry leaves shooting down my throat and making me feel sick.
I can taste clotted slime sliding down my throat.
I start to walk into the blood-red gunge.
I start to shout and scream.
My mum taps me on the hand, it was all a dream!

Stuart Davis (11)
Garendon High School

Hell

Devils killing
Demons eating
Screaming of dying children
Everlasting screeching
Burning flesh
Pitch-black smoke
Bubbling blood
Evil death
Horrible
School is hell!

Corey Muncie (11)
Garendon High School

Best Friends

Emily and I are best friends forever
Working together forever and ever
Best friends forever
Emily, Laura and I, best friends
Sticking together and helping each other always
Knowing each other for days and days
Best friends forever
Emily, Laura and I, best friends always
Having fun at sleepovers helps our friendship stay alive
Best friends forever and ever.

Rebecca Smith (11)
Garendon High School

Funky Fair

Enormous fast rides
Happy and joyful children
Scared people screaming
Delightful children laughing and playing
Sweet-smelling candyfloss
Yummy and fresh ice cream
Nasty smell of burning hot dogs
Fresh air and whistling wind
I feel great!

Zoe Wooldridge (12)
Garendon High School

The Castle In The Hills

The castle in the hills
Be ready for scary thrills
All covered in fog
With a guard dog
All rusted away
Dark and creepy doors come out to play
Beware, the castle in the hills!

Sarah Bajor (11)
Garendon High School

Cliff

The sea roaring funny words
The rocks so high under my feet
The seagulls speaking my secrets aloud
The sea attacking the rocks
The sun on my face, I have a lovely tan
The salty water I taste
I feel calm.

Chloe Lazell (11)
Garendon High School

At The Beach

I can see the sea swaying
And the children playing.

I can hear children laughing
And the trees whistling.

I can smell delicious ice cream
And the lovely fresh air.

I can taste a tasty juicy drink
And the horrible salty sea.

I can feel the wind blowing against my face.
I can feel the sand rubbing against my feet.

Emmie Bradshaw (11)
Garendon High School

Death Alley

Dirty litter bins going green.
Old fences starting to break.
Rats are squeaking in and out of the bins.
The wind slowly travelling down the valley.
The heat of the sun shining down on me.
Parts of fences off the ground.
Fresh air begins to rise.
Dust flying about all around me.
Horrible food smelling in the bins.
Rats are running away from me.

Leon Caine (11)
Garendon High School

Airplane

The silky sky.
The cushioned clouds.
The wind flies by me.
The birds so high.
The pressure on me.
The conscience gaining.
The fresh breathing air.
Warm chocolate tea beside me.
I feel lonely.

Emma Willis (11)
Garendon High School

Forest

Tall green beech tree.
Small cute fluffy animals.
Chirping off the tiny little bird.
Quick gusts of wind.
Beautiful long flowers.
Large raindrops falling on top of me.
Smell of rain.
The winter coming towards us.
The new fresh season coming my way.

Karishma Purshottam (11)
Garendon High School

Animals

Soft brown monkeys swinging from tree to tree.
Rough baby crocodiles swimming in the sea.
Singing birds flying in the sky.
Lion's roar, oh so loud when they're eating meat.
Saliva from the giraffes because they're eating leaves.
Hairy chimpanzees eating buckets of cheese.
I can hear the animals talking to me.

James Bullock (12)
Garendon High School

The Seaside

The calm ocean flowing.
The goldenness of the sand.
Waves hitting the rocks.
Eagles flying around.
The sand in my toes.
The blazing hot sun on my face.
Mint ice cream in my mouth.
The smell from the salt of the sea.
The smell from the café.

Nikita Thompson (11)
Garendon High School

The Park

Strong fencing surrounding me.
Sweet birds singing to me.
Fast cars speeding past me.
Weak branches blowing about in the wind.
Light breeze running through my hair.
Heat waves beating down.
But I still don't care!

Liam Start (12)
Garendon High School

The Free Kick

I looked at the ball
Then looked at the goal
I dreamt of the celebration
This was my goal

I started my run up
And looked at the wall
I saw they were scared
They knew it would hurt

I hit the ball
With all my might
My aim was true
With only five seconds left

It flew through the air
Like a bird to the sky
It was on target
I was on a high

A roar from the crowd
As it hit the net
I celebrated
It was one of my best.

Alastair Hawkins (13)
Garendon High School

Bully

'Bullied today
And tomorrow,'
Said the girl weeping in sorrow.

'They'll be back
They always are,'
Said the girl to her grandpa.

What did I do?
I do not see
Why you bully me.

Elizabeth Hickman (13)
Garendon High School

School Life - I Got Bullied

I travel to school, I look OK
But the kids take all my confidence away.
They call me names, they pull my hair,
They point at me and sneer and stare.
I just walk past; I hold my head high,
While something's there in the corner of my eye.
Two little sweet children playing a game,
I wish I was that young again.
To not get threatened, to not get hit,
To not get all these juicy little zits.
I feel like I get all the blame,
My life will never be the same.
The way it hurts all the time,
For no one cares about the feelings of mine.
I want to just fall down and cry,
For why, it's only me, oh why?
For the way I live, I'm all alone,
Cos all my parents do is moan.
I want to laugh, I wish to smile,
As I've been bullied for quite a while.
Afraid I am, I have no friends,
But by means no worry, I'm on the mends.
I just sit in my room, I lock the door
Before I turn on my dad's chainsaw.
I chop off my fingers, I chop off my toes,
For what I will chop off next, no one knows.

Shannon Checkley (13)
Garendon High School

Sport

I threw the ball as fast as I could,
It came back and hit me, I fell in the mud.
I kicked the ball down the pitch,
I tried to chase it but it gave me a stitch.
I ran a very long run
The worst bit was I was running in the sun.
I slogged the ball with all my might,
Suddenly the ball went out of sight.
In the tournament I was using front crawl,
After in the pub there was a right big brawl.
Sport is the best,
But now I need a rest!

Christopher Reeves (13)
Garendon High School

Life Today

On walls there is graffiti,
In streets there is some crime,
Is time going to stop like this
Forever in our lives?

The Earth is getting warmer,
The Poles are melting quicker,
Is time going to stop like this?
Ozone's not getting thicker!

Kidnaps and murders in our streets
Right in front of us,
Is time going to stop like this,
Nobody can tell!

People drinking, taking drugs
Why waste their lives,
I hope time doesn't stop like this
Because we only get one life!

Melissa Tombs (13)
Garendon High School

Summer's Week

On Monday all the children went out to play
On a hot beautiful summer's day.

On Tuesday the weather was cool,
But people went jumping in the swimming pool.

On Wednesday it was so hot
My parents drank the whole lot!

On Thursday we had a water fight,
I threw a water bomb with all my might.

On Friday we had a pizza
With my best friend Kizza.

On Saturday I was drawing round a bend
Knowing that the summer would end.

On Sunday I had a rest,
Our summers are the best.

Sam Haghighat (13)
Garendon High School

The Future Today

Books, videos, DVDs
All these new items,
Are the bees' knees.
What will we end up like?
Chrome, giants or birds,
Or will we turn into
Animals in herds?
What will we speak like?
English, Chinese or blurred,
Maybe even mind-reading,
With no language to be heard.
I've got to go now,
Back to my time,
All this wondering
Has stuck in my mind.

Daniel Day (13)
Garendon High School

Forest

Tall and green trees.
Small berry bushes.
Owls hooting.
Ferocious lions roaring.
Hot sun.
The wind brushing my face.
Fresh green leaves.
Cold raindrops.
Disgusting poos
And fresh grass.

Matthew Sanders (11)
Garendon High School

Forest

The tall green trees crashing through the air.
Small blackbirds chirping on the branches.
Huge hungry mammals roaring through the forest.
Feeling the wild wind rushing through my body.
Small raindrops that I can feel falling above my head.
The strong powerful wind, I can taste breathing.
The breath of fresh air getting colder and colder.
The great smell of the fresh wet grass blowing through the wind.

Sean Woolley (11)
Garendon High School

The Sky, The High Hill

High up in the sky
The sun shines right to my eyes.
The image of the breezy sea
Just keeps coming back to me.
Swiftly moving closer to me
And rushing back out to sea.

Up high on the hill
Sits a lady alone and still.
Muttering and rocking in her chair,
The church bells ring loud and clear
As she rocks upon the hill.

Hollie Cartwright (11)
Mount Grace High School

The Beautiful Beach

People along the sunlit sea
Sitting on sunbeds and drinking tea,
Lovers walking hand-in-hand
And children playing in the sand.

Fishers fishing on top of rocks
And jellyfish with ten-volt shocks,
Hermit crabs changing their shell
And little children collecting them well.

People in the sea with their snorkel and mask
Being a lifeguard isn't much of a task,
There are no sharks or fierce piranhas
Look some boats that look like bananas.

Then the day ends
And walking away families and friends,
The tide comes in and washes away
The remains of a nice long day.

Jacob Watson (11)
Mount Grace High School

Scars Make It Better

Secretly and silently
Cramming up your arm
Arranging the lines
Releasing the familiar harm
Smiling with joy
Making yourself feel pure
Aching to do it again
Keeping your own dirty secret
Engulfing all the pain
Ideal people call you a fool
Tell her what should she do
Believe in her, don't go
Everyone breaks her heart
Tell her, make her know
Treat her better than before
Ever wanted so much to hurt
Red blood, scars of worth.

Katherine Harris (14)
Mount Grace High School

Where Is Your Homework?

'Where is your homework?'
'Left it in France.'
'Where is your homework?'
'Dancing in France.'
'Where is your homework?'
'Dropped it in a pit.'
'Where is your homework?'
'It's really hard you have to admit.'
'Where is your homework?'
'Got struck by lightning.'
'Where is your homework?'
'My pen is very frightening.'
'Where is your homework?'
'Left it at my nan's.'
'Where is your homework?'
'Well, my mum had plans.'
'Where is your homework?'
'Chucked it away.'
'Where is your homework?'
'Miss, it was in for May.'
'Where is your homework?'
'Left it on the bus.'
'Where is your homework?'
'Stop making a fuss!'
'You have to do this homework, in for tomorrow or else!
Where is your homework?'
'Here it is with the extension too.'
'Oh well done, now 232 to go for all the homework that you didn't do.'
'Noooo!'

Joshua Stubberfield (12)
Mount Grace High School

Holocaust

To all those Jews who died
From Hitler's attempt at genocide
Dragged from your houses
Belongings taken including your best blouses
Held at gunpoint
Shot if you were to try to run away
So many of you had to stay.

Your families taken
Your children killed
I can't even imagine how you must have felt
Hurt, terrified, petrified, scared
The things you must have smelt
The things you must have heard
The things you must have seen
Must have been obscene
You got so thin
Your hair shaved off like animal skin.

Some of you died
By committing suicide
Taken to the death camps such as,
Auschwitz, Balzac, Sobibor, Chelmno, Majdanek and Treblinka
There you were gassed, starved, shot or diseased
After your bodies slunk on carts
Off to be burned.

You dug your own graves at gunpoint
Stood there with your children
Trying desperately to protect them in your arms
When you were shot dead, your body fell on them
And they were suffocated, they were far from harm.

You may have chosen to forgive but we will never forget
The evil, the suffering and the pain that you met.

Katie MacNaughton (14)
Mount Grace High School

Two Sides To Every Story
(Read the poem through, then read the 1st, 3rd, 5th line etc)

Love. The word bounced around inside my head,
I couldn't wait for the next day, the day we would be wed.
You said you loved me, I believed you too,
But friends said that I was way too young to say, I do.
Lie, a lie it was, you and me were great together,
Arguments, lying between you and me happened never.
For rows, punch-ups and fights,
We never experienced, together we were a shining light.

You reached into the closet; it was dim and dark,
Then in your hand something let out a spark.
I saw something, bright, shiny, glimmering,
A beautiful gold necklace gorgeous and shimmering,
You brought it round up to my neck with delight,
I was blessed and felt like a soaring kite.
You slid it along with a grin on your face,
And fastened it up at a dream pace.

Then there was music, a miraculous sound,
As we glided down the aisle, my true love I had found.
I felt like I was floating in an amazing way,
We then said our I dos like you say.
I looked down now to see the old me,
Now it was you and me, we.
A knife right straight through a broken heart,
That could never happen now; nothing could tear us apart,
I thought nothing could tear us apart.

Kelly Ward (13)
Mount Grace High School

How Sweet To Be A Cloud

How sweet to be a little cloud
Floating in the blue,
Every little cloud
Always sings aloud.

How sweet to be a cloud
Floating in the blue
It makes him very proud
To be a little cloud!

Danielle Smith (11)
Mount Grace High School

My Life

My life was hard, my life was tough
I found those days so long and rough
My mother here, my father there
I'm in the middle but they don't care!
I love my grandma, she loves me
Now we're together, happy as can be!

Lorna Pacey (11)
Mount Grace High School

Family And Friends

If you are feeling happy
If you are feeling sad, confused
If you are feeling conned
If you need help
Family and friends are there for you.

Amy Pacey (13)
Mount Grace High School

Poetry

Tell me, tell me
Tell me now,
Where and when
And who and how.

Why do people ruin our lives?
Why do bees live in hives?

Tell me, tell me,
Tell me now,
Where and when
And who and how.

Why do people always grow old?
Why is the North Pole so cold?

Tell me, tell me,
Tell me now,
Where and when
And who and how.

Why do people go to sleep in a bed?
Why is the sun so red?

Taylor Crisp (11)
Mount Grace High School

Love, Love, Love

The perfect feeling,
Full of happiness
But my heart's bleeding,
My feelings are weak, full of worry, things are too good,
It's not a feeling, it's love.

Ever been in love?

My answer was no,
That's why I was scared,
Afraid, lost in my own mind,
Love means loss of identity,
Once lost, it's hard to find.

So I'm here, brainwashed,
Obsessed with my lover,
I doubt I will ever find another,
Hence why I'm afraid,
Not getting anywhere in this world,
Split into two, love against my mind,
My heart's blind
But I'm carrying on till I find
Myself once again.

Ever realised someone doesn't feel the same?
I have, but I'm telling no name,
That's the idea of love, it's a game,
You give and take,
Finally one day you'll win
Where I'll see you at the end.

Rebecca Hindmarch (16)
The Rutland College

Dancing Shoes

A childhood memory
Of love and devotion.
A lifetime of happiness
Shattered.

Red, yellow, blue green.
A palette of colours will no longer be seen
On a dance floor of dreams.

Lines in the mirror stare back at me.
Pointed toes and jazz hands fail to please
An artist in disguise
As never-ending ribbons stream.

With a glimmer of hope, then darkness
Realisation sets in.
Boxes packed. Tissues strewn
And a fairytale is no more.

Natasha Schofield (16)
The Rutland College

The Two Sisters

Two peas in a pod,
Sisters in our heads,
Share each other's burdens,
Happy and at peace.

Stories of past times,
Distant,
Time spent in each other's company,
Fading,
Seeing them and their true colours,
Disappointing.

Bitter fights unleash cans of worms,
Reason strong in the mind
Weak at the crunch.
Memories locked away never to be opened,
Happiness turns bitter.
Trust, loyalty becomes betrayal and ignorance
Sadness over-powered by its enemy,
Anger.

A lit candle now just a burnt out wick
The aftermath like that of a war,
Silence.

So I know this person. Who are they to me?
Just a fading past,
A block of the past dissolving
Replaced by new adventures.

No longer doubts floating around head and heart.
Mentally physically and emotionally drained.

Do or did you say what you mean?
Did you or do you mean what you say?
Like a ship floating to its end.
They two sisters,
Broke.

Keri Mowat (16)
The Rutland College

The Stars In Her Eyes

Hold back the sun from rising,
For I can see the stars in her eyes.
Hold back the rain from falling,
Just let us keep this moment in time.
I feel like I'm losing my best friend,
And there's nothing I can do to stop it,
I look in her eyes and see a tear start to fall,
If you won't give me this night to remember,
Please give me it all.

She's standing here in front of me as we stand by her front door.
I don't know what to say to her, that hasn't been said before.
I pull her close and put her head against mine,
Wishing we could keep this moment in time.
She kisses me on the cheek and starts to open the door,
I see her suitcases, packed and stacked up on the floor.
My heart skips a beat, as I look in her bright eyes again,
Will I ever see her again? And if so . . . when?

She can tell that something is wrong, she knows me far too well.
I know she's feeling the same way, but she doesn't want to say.
I pull her close again; she says she doesn't want to leave.
I tell her it'll all be fine and that I'll love her more each day.
She gives me that perfect smile, the kind that makes me melt.
Why it's taken all this time to tell her how I've felt?
She takes my hand as she steps inside; I wonder what she'll say,
Her eyes so bright, her smile so perfect, I just wish that she could stay.
That night had been amazing and the rain began to fall,
I don't want a moment to remember her, I'll remember it all.

Chris White (18)
The Rutland College

Who Says Blondes Have More Fun?

With her long blonde hair and blue eyes,
All the boys stared as she walked by.
Everyone thought it,
It wasn't just you.
She did have a smile on her face,
You were right,
But she told me she was dying inside.
She did have a pretty face,
And yes, all the boys did like her.
Where did it all go wrong?
Is the question people were asking
As they stood in the street
And watched the coffin go by.

Amii Slater (16)
The Rutland College

Untitled

They own your heart,
They pull on your strings,
No matter what
They always win.

Walls come crashing down,
Ancient defences upturned,
What used to be is not anymore,
Everything on the edge.

They own your heart,
They pull on your strings.
No matter what
They always win.

Some say they'll protect us,
Some say we're safe,
But really it's an illusion,
Everything on the edge.

They own your heart,
They pull on your strings,
No matter what
They always win.

Planning when to strike,
Our lives in their hands,
What will happen this time?
Nothing in our control.

They own your heart,
They pull on your strings,
No matter what
They always win.

Attacks on faith?
Attacks for greed?
Why is this happening?
Nothing in our control.

They own your heart,
They pull on your strings,
No matter what
They always win.

Masochism, lunacism, anger and hate,
This is still the big debate,
The world is full of hopes and fears,
Let's just hope it doesn't end in tears.

Elizabeth Blades (16)
The Rutland College

Seven Months

You look at me, big brown eyes,
Staring.
You hold onto me, soft gentle hands,
Grasping.
You're not perfect, no one is.
Two extra fingers, one extra toe.
Seven months you've looked at me,
Those big brown eyes staring.
Seven months you've held onto me,
Those soft gentle hands grasping.
You're not perfect, no one is.
Waking in the night, three, four times.
You laugh,
High laugh,
Low laugh,
You are perfect.
You rely on us, now we rely on you.
Just seven months you've been with us.
Those big brown eyes staring,
Those soft gently hands grasping.
Just seven months,
Now we rely on you like you rely on us.

Cheryl Freestone (17)
The Rutland College

Him

He's always there
Everywhere I go
When I'm happy or sad
He's always there to taunt me.

But I can't live without him
And he can't live without me
We'd die without each other
That is how we live together.

Suffocating me around others
Beneath the surface I'm quietly dealing
With his words that hurt me
Only he can truly hurt me.

The only refuge I have is song
He is speechless when I sing
He cannot bear to listen.
I have control
Because then I can hurt him too.

David Rattenbury (17)
The Rutland College

War

Seventy years past, the time I signed,
The family I left who cried and whined.
To war I was heading, to battle I was going,
Death was growing, as all were knowing.
Bombs were like raindrops falling from above,
Bullets like showers impossible to touch.
Men I killed, the laws were broken,
God looked on, to all that was spoken.
As I lay there tears burning in my eyes,
A piece of shrapnel came falling from the sky.
It hit me hard and struck me down,
And when I woke up I looked around.
Sixteen years I was when I died,
For freedom, for love, we came and tried.
In the palace of angels is where I lie,
For others to fight, to try, to die.

Marc Garley (16)
The Rutland College

Not A Good Poem

The paper mocks
The pen, unused
There is nothing to write
And I tear up the pieces of the previous disaster
They flutter like fallen snow
The colour is the same as my thoughts
Blank
I'm desperate now, so desperate
I call for help in my mind
But my muse has
Gone out for lunch
A good time to desert me
No more thank you cards for her
An old enemy to struggle with
I draw my sword and prepare to duel
Despite my best efforts though
My adversary is formidable
And with a final thrust he flings away my sword
One-nil
Back to reality
No closer to an idea
'There is nothing scarier than an empty page,'
A poet once said
And now I know what he meant.

Sophie Morgan (16)
The Rutland College

The Circle Of Life

It is spring and life begins.
Newborn lambs bounce joyfully around in the clean fresh air
While beautiful blossom blooms on trees
And birds sing songs of love.

The hot summer's sun beats down on the swan
As she swims in the lake with her signets.
The crystal white horses having the time of their lives
Gallop as cattle and sheep lie in the grass and graze contentedly.

Now, summer has gone
And the birds have flown, too
Because winter is fast approaching.
The leaves from the trees now lay on the ground
Whilst animals prepare for the cold times ahead.

A deer wanders aimlessly.
In search of scraps for survival.
Under a dusting of white, hidden away is a tree
Which was once filled with love songs and life.
It is silent.

Rebecca Williams (16)
The Rutland College

Do You Love Her?

Female, woman,
Love her, hate her
Respect her,
Wouldn't you?
So beautiful,
Isn't she?

Could you love her?
Well, could you?

A creation of God,
Special, meaningful.
Full of feelings,
Unleashed in an instant.
She lures you,
Me, too look,
To wish,
To want her.

Will you ever love her?
Well, could you?

One look could be the last,
While two is tempting,
Watch her tempting you,
Testing you.

Have you ever loved her?
Well, could you?

She's an angel,
Full of grace,
Full of perfection,
So peaceful,
Calming,
So satisfying.

Could you turn her down?
Well, could you?

Do you love her?
She is the description of evil.

Sean Goff (16)
The Rutland College

Slow Dance

I held you close to me, cheek-to-cheek,
I felt your breath melt on my skin,
So warm, so full of life,
As we moved to the music and danced the slow dance.

Later, we went home, our heads swam with memories,
Uncontrollable emotions, indeterminable thoughts,
As we held each other close,
And we moved to the music of life,
Dancing the slow dance of passion.

Time passed, I visited you as often as I would dare,
Didn't want to be over possessive,
But that day something was wrong,
There was no warm greeting, no welcoming arms,
There was no sound at all,
Just silence, the music of a world,
That waits with its breath withheld,
No slow dance awaiting me.

I found you lying on your bed,
Under velvet sheets, your skin was pale, waxy,
Your eyes glazed, I held you close to me,
Felt your breath on my neck so cold,
Void of the life that once resided,
I sung under my breath and we swayed, slowly,
Ever so slowly to the melody and I felt the change,
As the slow dance of fate stole you away from me.

My time will come one day,
As yours already had, too early,
I'll be cold, like you, empty,
My hourglass will run still,
And then we can move to the music once more,
To the sound of harps, a slow dance of eternity,
Locked forever in bliss,
A slow dance of life and death that will never end.

Graham Nice (17)
The Rutland College

Autumn Leaves

I walked through the park, past the trees whose leaves were falling off
And being blown away by the wind,
It was getting colder than before.
I couldn't wear any more T-shirts and shorts now,
It was scarves and woolly hats.
Winter was drawing nearer.
Crispy cold, yet sunny as I walked down the path,
My dog running in front chasing after a ball,
Unperturbed by the colder weather.

I ambled through the leafy park,
Along cracked pavement stones littered with leaves,
All dead, crispy and crumpled,
Being blown from branches of semi-clothed trees.

The wind raced past my face and ears,
Running her icy fingers through my hair,
She whistled her tune as she went,
Unwrapping my scarf in a playful dare.

The cold crisp air condenses my breath,
And crawls under my clothes to chill my skin,
The summer warmth is dead and gone,
We are just left in wait for winter to begin.

The wind, she has a job to do,
She capably clears up skeletal leaves,
Sweeps them up to blow them away,
She hides our summer with a breeze.

Still the sun shines on evermore,
Despite the biting cold air.
But now the only warmth we feel,
Is from the coloured leaves that trees still wear.

Gemma Ryan (16)
The Rutland College

Loveable Limericks

There once was a neglected dog called Token
Who lived in a town called Oakham.
He dug up a bone,
And took it straight home,
Where his owner tried to choke him.

In a little village called Gunthorpe,
Laid a miniature bottle of port.
A kid came and drunk it,
Fell over his drum kit,
What a stupid thing, he thought.

There once was a cow that peeled
Who lived in a dingy field.
An elf passed by,
Pretended to fly,
And *poof* the cow was healed.

I end with a piece of cheese
An addict he would tease.
It melted in a pan,
The addict, he ran,
Tripped and scraped his knees.

Anna Diffey (16)
The Rutland College

Empty Space

An empty space
Of tales unknown
Are we marbles or are we dolls?
It is a fact unknown
In an empty space.

An empty space
Known only to you
Are you watching me?
Insignificant to you
In an empty space.

A empty space
I didn't think you real
Is it just me that knows of you?
I'm not sure of anything real
In an empty space.

I walked across
An empty space
Have I met you before?
You know the pathway like you know my life
I felt the air of an empty space.

Since you know my life
In that empty space
Could I not have had a better life to lead?
You have everything, yet nothing
Up there in that empty space.

Phoebe Harris (16)
The Rutland College

Lies I Told My Internet Boyfriend

I lied on the Internet to him and said I was six-foot two
And then I told him that my boobs were new,
I hinted that I was size eight and had dark eyes
I saw no harm in these little white lies.

I let him believe that I was blonde and pretty
And then I stole quotes from the Net to make me look witty,
I pretended to be elegant and extremely well dressed
When I said I could speak French he seemed very impressed.

I implied that I could play the piano and that I regularly ran
And that's when it all stopped going according to plan,
He sent me an email and said I was too good to be true
And that he was desperate to meet me more than I knew.

A problem has risen because the moment we meet
He'll realise the only thing about size eight are my feet,
He's bound to notice that I ever so slightly lied over the Net
Some of which now I am starting to regret.

The complete truth is and it pains me to say
As he will surely spot in the harsh light of day,
My legs aren't exactly endless and the worst of it all
It's crystal clear that I'm nowhere near six-foot tall.

And all that's left to do is to email my hapless Romeo
To say that before the big day there's something he should know,
Juliet, when describing herself missed off the odd pound
And in non-virtual reality looks decidedly round!

Amy Bell (16)
The Rutland College

Succubus Love

Fantasy, sex, in my life I'll disdain
My lover of faith and his lover of pain,
My lover, this taste of the blood on the blade
Once and again you will lead me astray.

Sanctuary yields in your pyreous flame,
Your tongue on the air, my rebellion will tame,
The funeral pyre from the lights in the sky,
Memories gone in the glint of an eye.

Whisper the fog, deep into my mind
The cool of the wind in winter so kind,
Continue my words as they bite at my ear
Consequence bites into the remnants of fear.

Alan Young (18)
The Rutland College

Love Sonnet

Your magical blue eyes and dark brown hair,
Your love lifts me up on a small white cloud.
Your strength is so strong and you are so fair,
And when I'm with you, you make me so proud.
You treat me like a small fragile flower,
Your scent is a fragrance I can float on.
We can conquer the world with our power,
Our love will be able to go on strong.
From where I reflect your heavenly smile,
Thanking my stars for leading me to you.
We walk in the moonlight for miles and miles,
Before I knew a love could be so true.
So I send to you this delicate rhyme,
With love and thanks to be yours and you mine.

Jennifer Griggs (16)
The Rutland College

Who

Who is the person that picks you up
When life is getting you down?
Who will always be there for you
And bring out the magic you own?
Who is always going to be around
No matter what life throws your way?

Who can bring out your deepest desires
And make you seek your dream?
Who has the ability to make you weak
And the power to make you strong?
And who will always be there for you
No matter where you go wrong?

Who can truly say that they are yours
And you are truly theirs?
Your friends, your family, your lover,
Your soulmate.

Carly Brown (17)
The Rutland College

The Altruistic Apple!

The life of an apple is a simple tale,
A carefree existence on high,
There's no worries to earn or to clothe itself,
It's as easy as a piece of apple pie.

For our little green apple friend, Rock-Steady-Eddie,
Life was like living a dream,
He'd sit all day long and soak up the sun,
Happy and free it would seem.

On a hot summer's day when the wind was gentle,
Came a man with long curly hair,
With a rugged look, Sir Isaac Newton stood,
And took a deep breath of fresh air.

He then sat in the shade and sighed to himself,
With a confused and slight anxious look,
Meanwhile Steady Eddie was intrigued from up high,
When a thought then suddenly struck.

I must help this poor man and be at his side,
But first I must wriggle me free!
So he twisted and turned but did not come loose,
It simply wasn't destined to be.

One warm autumn's day, a big gale blew past,
Blistering and howling itself by,
Eddie thought to himself that this was his chance,
And with effort he fell from up high.

Sacrificing his life, Eddie helped with mankind,
'Cause his fall was Isaac's new view,
The tale of an apple you'd think was quite simple,
But for Eddie, that wasn't quite true.

Maria Walmsley (16)
The Rutland College

What Is Life When It Becomes Nothing

Me
A meaningless speck of dirt,
A strand of barbed wire woven amongst the purest thread.
A black snowflake swallowed by the white virgin snow.

I'm left waiting for something destined never to arrive.
Wading through a river of feelings I melt,
And I'm washed away with the current.

Breathing never felt so wrong.
The elements of perfect animosity,
Together now they destroy my being.

This, like a song absent of words of music.
Standing in a storm of emotion I crumble to dust,
And I'm blown away in the wind.

This will never be resolved.
There is always me
And although my exterior is utterly shattered,
Inside only my heart is breaking.

Matt Howlett (16)
The Rutland College

Young Writers Information

We hope you have enjoyed reading this book - and that you will continue to enjoy it in the coming years.

If you like reading and writing poetry drop us a line, or give us a call, and we'll send you a free information pack.

Alternatively if you would like to order further copies of this book or any of our other titles, then please give us a call or log onto our website at www.youngwriters.co.uk

**Young Writers Information
Remus House
Coltsfoot Drive
Peterborough
PE2 9JX**

(01733) 890066